HIGH LEVEL STRATEGY FOR THE TOEIC® L&R TEST

800点を目指すTOEIC® L&R TEST演習

Emiko Matsumoto / Kento Inoue / Graciella Bautista

SANSHUSHA

はじめに

★ 本書で学ぶ皆さんへ ★

理由はあとからついてくる

　突然ですが、皆さんは自分が小さかったときのことを覚えていますか。「道の向こうから車が走って近づいてきたら、自分が今いる場所からよけて、車との衝突を避けなければいけない」と学んだときのことを。

　そのときはきっと、お父さんお母さんか他の誰かが、あなたに教えてくれたはずです。「車が近づいてきたら、よけないといけませんよ」と。そのときは、お父さん、お母さんの言っている意味はわからず叱られていると感じたかもしれないけれど、あなたを大切にしてくれる誰かが、あなたに真剣に言ってくれている。だからあなたは「言うことをきこう」と思いました。「車が来たら、よけないといけないんだ。だって、怒られるから」。そうやって、あなたは車に近づかないことを学んだのかもしれませんね。

　でも、時間が経ってからわかりましたよね。「走って近づいてきている車からは危険だからよける」と。そして、成長したあなたはそのことを、大切な弟さんや妹さん、小さな親戚に教えたはずです。これから将来、守るべき家族ができたら、皆さんがそれを大切な誰かに教えていくでしょう。

　皆さんを含む多くの人は最初に「強制される」ことには何らかの抵抗を感じるものです。人から何かを強制される言葉には抵抗を感じるでしょう。例えば、

「早く起きなさい」

「勉強しなさい」

「今日はそんな本を読んでいないで、試験勉強をしなさい」

「先生のまえでは礼儀正しくしなさい」

「あなたが悪いのだから、先輩に謝りなさい」など。

　それに抵抗する気持ちには理由があるはずです。

「今勉強しようとしていたのに」

「集中力を高めるために、今は別の本を読みたかった」

「別に嫌われてもいい、自分が悪くもないのに頭を下げたくない」など。

　でも一方、すべてを自主的に考えて行動するよりも、ある程度は行動を決められていた方が、楽だと思うこともあるでしょう。行動を決められているからできること、例えば、

「学校があるから、早起きできる」

「試験があるから、勉強できる」
「信号があるから、みんなが安全に道路を使用できる」
「マニュアルどおりに謝ってみたら、人間関係が改善した」などです。

　しかし、その「強制」というのは、最初は命令だったかもしれませんが、次第に自然と身についてしまうこともあるでしょう。毎日の生活の中で、口に出してはっきりと「命令」、または「強制」されることもありますが、多くは
「昔、親に強制されたから、それを続けているだけ」
「何となく、先生に監視されている気がするから、遅刻をしないようにする」
「なんとなく、交番がそこにあるから、信号を守る」
と、何となく、誰かの管理下に自分を置いていることもあるかもしれません。

　そして次第に「管理されている」という意識はなくなって、あなたは自主的に行動していると思っているかもしれません。
「好きな友達と会いたいから、学校に早く到着する」
「一緒に横断歩道を渡っているおばあさんのことを気にしながら、交通ルールを守ってみる」
「勉強したいから勉強する」
「自分が主導権をとるために先に謝ってしまう」
などと、自分の意志で、行動することもあるでしょう。
　言われたからやっているのか、自分から行動しているのか、その線引きというのは複雑で、一日のすべての行動のどれもこれもに、白黒つけることはできないでしょう。

　私はここで、「自主的に勉強しよう」と、みなさんに熱く語るつもりはありません。
　皆さんはすでに「自主的に勉強すること」の楽しさはわかっているからです。

　それよりも、**何かを強制されて、仕方なくやっているとき、そこに罪悪感を覚えないでください。と私は皆さんにお伝えしたい。何かを義務感で仕方なくやっている、そんなあなたの行動は素晴らしいと私は思います。**
　いつか、今やっている行動の意味が、すっと腑に落ちてくるときが来ると思います。
そして、「そのとき」はあなたが想像しているよりもずっと早くやってきます。今のあなたを、きっとそのときのあなたは、応援してくれているはずです。
　皆さんが英語学習をとおして、少しでも幸せな将来に近づくことを、心よりお祈りしています。

著者代表　松本恵美子

本書の特長

　本書は TOEIC® 中級者から上級者のための大学の授業でのテキストです。TOEIC® LISTENING AND READING TEST のスコアアップに必要な基礎力と応用力を身に付けることを目的に編集されました。2016 年から導入されている現在のテスト形式に対応しています。1 ユニットですべてのパートの練習をすることができるように組み立てられており、授業進度に応じて、1 ユニット進むのに 1 コマ、もしくは 2 コマ以上の時間をかけてもよいでしょう。授業内の短時間で TOEIC® 形式の問題に慣れ、解答のコツを身に付けながら実践問題に親しむことができます。

本書の構成と特長

① 全 15 ユニット構成、Unit 1 ～ 14 の各ユニットの問題数は全 30 問
　各ユニット、Part 1（2 問）、Part 2（4 問）、Part 3（3 問）、Part 4（3 問）、Part 5（9 問）、Part 6（4 問）、Part 7（5 問）の全 30 問となっており、1 つのユニットで Part 1 ～ Part 7 までの実践問題が学習できます。
② Unit 1 ～ 14 の各ユニットの始めには Vocabulary Check
　そのユニットに関連した単語を最初に学習することができます（15 語）。
③ Unit 15 はミニテストで問題数は全 35 問
　ミニテストは Part 1（4 問）、Part 2（6 問）、Part 3（3 問）、Part 4（3 問）、Part 5（10 問）、Part 6（4 問）、Part 7（5 問）の全 35 問となっています。
④ 教授用資料としてリスニング・スクリプトの穴埋め問題、単語テスト
　授業用の資料として、リスニングの全スクリプトと、その穴埋め問題、単語テストを用意しています。

　作成にあたり、Unit 1 ～ Unit 14 の Vocabulary Check、Unit 1 ～ Unit 15 の Part 1、Part 2、Part 3、Part 4、Part 6、Part 7 の解説と、Unit 1、Unit 2 の問題作成、全体の監修を松本が、Part 5 の解説と問題作成を井上が、Unit 1~Unit 15 の Part 3、Part 4、Part 6、Part 7 の問題作成と全体の英文校正を Bautista が担当しました。本書を効果的に活用され、TOEIC® スコアアップのための英語力を身に付けられることを心より祈っております。

Contents

音声ダウンロード＆ストリーミングサービス（無料）のご案内

https://www.sanshusha.co.jp/text/onsei/isbn/9784384335217/

本書の音声データは、上記アドレスよりダウンロードおよびストリーミング再生ができます。ぜひご利用ください。

Download

Streaming

Restaurant

Vocabulary Check!

Choose an appropriate translation for the following words.

🔊 01

1. alternative ( )	**2.** personally ( )	**3.** resume ( )
4. dough ( )	**5.** diner ( )	**6.** authentic ( )
7. aftermath ( )	**8.** booklet ( )	**9.** marinated ( )
10. organic ( )	**11.** pandemic ( )	**12.** cuisine ( )
13. confidential ( )	**14.** vegan ( )	**15.** complimentary ( )

a. 酢漬けにした	b. 余波	c. 秘伝の	d. 世界的に大流行している感染症
e. 無料の	f. 料理	g. 代替の	h. ビーガン
i. 冊子	j. 再開する	k. 生地	l. 真正の
m. 有機の	n. 個人的に	o. 食事客	

🎧 Listening Section

Part 1 Photographs

Strategy for Part 1 ［写真描写問題の解き方］

人物 1 人の写真

　人物が 1 人だけ写っている写真、または 1 人の人物にフォーカスを当てている場合は、選択肢の主語はすべて同じ語（He，She，The man，A woman など）であることが多いです。写真の人物が 1 人の場合、選択肢の主語がすべて同じかどうか、確認してみましょう。

1. 🔊 02

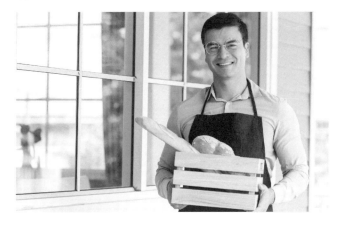

Ⓐ Ⓑ Ⓒ Ⓓ

2.

Ⓐ Ⓑ Ⓒ Ⓓ

Part 2 **Question-Response**

Strategy for Part 2 ［応答問題の解き方］

疑問詞で始まる疑問文 ①　Where, Who, When

　Part 2 の設問の半分以上は 5 W 1 H の疑問詞で始まる疑問文です。まず、文頭の What / When / Where / Who / Why / How を聞き取り、それを忘れないように記憶しておきましょう。

🔊 03

3.　Mark your answer on your answer sheet.　　Ⓐ Ⓑ Ⓒ

4.　Mark your answer on your answer sheet.　　Ⓐ Ⓑ Ⓒ

5.　Mark your answer on your answer sheet.　　Ⓐ Ⓑ Ⓒ

6.　Mark your answer on your answer sheet.　　Ⓐ Ⓑ Ⓒ

Questions 7-9   ◀)) 04

7.　When is the event?

(A) Monday morning

(B) Monday evening

(C) Friday morning

(D) Friday evening

8.　What does the woman need to accomplish?

(A) Some documents

(B) A documentary

(C) An incident report

(D) Some procurement files

9.　What will the woman do next?

(A) Skip work

(B) Finish her food

(C) Fulfill her task

(D) Invite a colleague

Part 4 Talks

Strategy for Part 4 ［説明文問題の解き方］

　Listening Section の４つのパートのうち、Part 4 を苦手とする人が比較的多いようです。語彙の難易度が高く、問題文も長い傾向にあるので、聞き取りが困難に感じるのでしょう。しかし、説明文のテーマは限られていますので、冒頭に集中して聞くと話の内容がわかります。

Questions 10-12　　　　　　　　　　　　　　　　　　　　　　　🔊 05

10. What is the event being talked about?

(A) A food exhibit

(B) A market sale

(C) A shop's opening

(D) A grand closing sale

11. Who does the speaker consider upon making the restaurant's concept?

(A) Non-meat eaters

(B) Meat-eaters

(C) People on diet

(D) Vegetable farmers

12. What does the restaurant offer to today's diners?

(A) A free dish

(B) A special seat

(C) A discount

(D) A coupon

Part 5　Incomplete Sentences

Strategy for Part 5 ［短文穴埋め問題の解き方］

　短文穴埋め問題では、問題タイプをすばやく判断することがとても重要です。すべての問題に均等に時間を費やすのではなく、時間を割くべき設問とそうでない設問を見極めましょう。問題を解き始める前に必ず選択肢を確認して、以下の4つの種類を判別しましょう。

問題タイプ	解答目安	本書での掲載ユニット
品詞識別問題	5 ～ 15 秒	UNIT 1
語彙問題	10 ～ 20 秒	UNIT 2 - UNIT 3
動詞（時制）問題	15 ～ 30 秒	UNIT 4 - UNIT 7
文法問題	15 ～ 30 秒	UNIT 8 - UNIT 14

【品詞識別問題】

　英文をすべて読まなくても、空所の前後と選択肢を見れば解ける品詞識別問題は、Part 5 の代表的な問題です。選択肢には、語幹（変化しない語形）と派生語（接頭辞や接尾辞が付加された語形）が並び、時制を含む語（動詞）が含まれていないのが特徴です。「前後がこの品詞なら、空所にはこの品詞しか当てはまらない」という判断が重要になります。「文の要素」と「品詞の機能」の基本的な知識が必須になるので、ここで学習していきましょう。

「文の要素」

Subject 〈主語〉	文の動作主になる名詞または名詞と同じような働きをする語
Verb 〈動詞〉	◆自動詞　主語にだけ影響が及ぶ行為や作用を表す動詞 　　　　　（例：go, swim, sleep など） ◇他動詞　主語が他に影響を及ぼす行為や作用を表す動詞 　　　　　（例：make, love, put など）
Object 〈目的語〉	他動詞の対象（〜に）や目的（〜を）を表す語
Complement 〈補語〉	主語や目的語の性質や状態を説明する語

「品詞の機能」

名詞	「人」「場所」「物」「事柄」を表す。（代名詞は名詞を置き換えた語） 〖可能な文の要素〗主語、他動詞の目的語、前置詞の目的語、補語
形容詞	名詞を修飾し、「どのような（どんな）」性質や状態かを説明する。 〖可能な文の要素〗補語　＊「形容詞＋名詞」は、名詞の機能に従う。
副詞	名詞以外を修飾し、様態や程度、頻度、時、場所を付加的に描写する。 〖可能な文の要素〗なし

例題 The new tablet model sold ------- because it outperformed its competitors in terms of battery durability.

    (A) success   (B) successfully   (C) succeed   (D) successful

解説 空所の前に動詞 sold があるため、これ以上動詞は入りません。(C) succeed を入れると動詞が重複することになります。(A) success は名詞なので、自動詞 sold の後ろに置くことができません。(D) successful は形容詞で、動詞や文を修飾できません。したがって、動詞 sold を修飾できる副詞 (B) successfully が正解です。

★接続詞（because）は新たな SV（文）を導いてしまい、空所の役割を考えるうえでは重要ではありません。まずは、**空所を含む文や節に着目**しましょう。

参考訳 バッテリー持続性において他社機種を上回ったので、新型タブレットはよく売れた。

13. Customer reviews revealed that the online reservation system was unnecessarily -------.

(A) complicates
(B) complicatedly
(C) complicated
(D) complication

14. One of Ms. Baxter's primary duties is to offer regular customers a ------- copy of her restaurant's recipes to commemorate the 10th anniversary of opening.

(A) complimentary
(B) compliments
(C) compliment
(D) complimentarily

15. Simon Park's dishes ------- combine traditional ingredients with modern techniques.

(A) skill   (B) skilled   (C) skillfully   (D) skillful

16. Since seasonal specials are renewed every three months, Mr. Greg has to design flyers for ------- to potential customers.

(A) distribution   (B) distribute   (C) distributive   (D) distributor

17. Oliver's Retail is a ------- retail store to provide fresh and nutritious produce.

(A) rely   (B) reliance   (C) reliably   (D) reliable

18. The aftermaths of the pandemic ------- longer than the restaurant owner expected.

(A) lasts   (B) lasted   (C) lastly   (D) lasting

19. The number of customers has ------- grown since the new campaign began last month.

(A) steadily   (B) steadiest   (C) steady   (D) steadiness

20. The owner is expecting more nutritious fruits as a result of ------- weather conditions.

(A) favors   (B) favorable   (C) favor   (D) favorably

21. The restaurant sold unused cookwares with ------- safety booklets attached to them.

(A) comprehensive
(B) comprehends
(C) comprehension
(D) comprehensively

Part 6　Text Completion

Question 22-25 refer to the following announcement.

Thanksgiving Holiday Announcement

Dear Valued Customers,

We would like to inform you that Rich Table restaurant will be closed from November 20th until the 24th (Monday to Friday) for this year's Thanksgiving holiday. We highly ------- everyone to place their takeaway orders on or before
22.
the 17th and they will be scheduled for ------- on the 18th and 19th (Saturday and
23.
Sunday). -------.
24.
We hope for your ------- and we wish you a happy and relaxing Thanksgiving with
25.
your loved ones!

---

22. (A) inspire　　(B) refer　　(C) encourage　　(D) initiate

23. (A) delivery　　(B) deliver　　(C) deliverable　　(D) deliverance

24. (A) This is our company's policy.
    (B) It will be busy on Thanksgiving week.
    (C) This will be on a first-come, first-served basis.
    (D) We will resume operations on those days.

25. (A) concern　　(B) refreshment　　(C) patronage　　(D) understanding

Strategy for Part 7 ［読解問題の解き方］

TOEIC の Part 7 は「読解問題」です。パッセージが計 15 個、54 問から成っています。Part 7 全体で約 55 分以上の時間を使えるように、まずは時間配分に気を付けて練習しましょう。

Questions 26-30 refer to the following advertisement.

De Luca's Pizzeria

Get a taste of Italy in New York!

We have been serving authentic Italian pizza since Antonio De Luca opened the original restaurant in a modest shop in Greenport. Thirty years later, his children and grandchildren continue to craft delectable pizza using traditional Italian techniques of kneading dough and De Luca's secret sauce.

We offer dine-in, carryout, and delivery service within miles of our locations.

All Neapolitan pizzas are created made-to-order, to guarantee freshness, and include your choice of three Italian toppings. Every pizza is served with a large beverage and two pieces of Focaccia bread.

A selection of salads and pastas are available as side dishes.

All vegetable toppings are local, certified organic, and farm-to-table.

We have De Luca Branches in the following locations:

Brooklyn

Manhattan

Queens

Greenport

Call us at +1-718-8975-899 and get a 5% discount on your first order.

We are open from 9:00 A.M. to 6:00 P.M on Wednesdays and Thursdays, and 9:00 A.M. to 7:00 P.M on Fridays to Sundays.

---

26. What does De Luca's Pizzeria claim about their food?

(A) They serve genuine Italian cuisine.

(B) They cater to American taste.

(C) Their food is unpredictable.

(D) They import pizza from Italy.

27. What is true about De Luca's Greenport shop?

(A) It has recently expanded.

(B) It is under new management.

(C) It does not offer delivery.

(D) It was the first location to open.

28. What is indicated about De Luca's pizzas?

(A) They are reasonably priced.

(B) They are imported from Italy.

(C) Their sauce is confidential.

(D) Their vegetable toppings come from De Luca-owned farms.

29. What is NOT included with a Neapolitan pizza?

(A) Flat Bread

(B) Pasta

(C) Toppings

(D) Drinks

30. How many days does the pizzeria operate?

(A) 4 days

(B) 5 days

(C) 6 days

(D) 7 days

UNIT 2

Sightseeing

Vocabulary Check!

Choose an appropriate translation for the following words.

🔊 06

1. occasionally ( )	2. regulation ( )	3. sculpture ( )
4. vacant ( )	5. showcase ( )	6. exhibition ( )
7. affordable ( )	8. competition ( )	9. attempt ( )
10. reputable ( )	11. performance ( )	12. completely ( )
13. donation ( )	14. recommend ( )	15. backpack ( )

a. 彫刻	b. 完全に	c. 試み	d. 競争、大会
e. リュックサック	f. 時々	g. 著名な	h. 寄付
i. 展覧会	j. 陳列棚、展示する	k. 勧める	l. 実演
m. 手ごろな	n. 空（から）の	o. 規定	

🎧 Listening Section

Part 1　Photographs

Strategy for Part 1 ［写真描写問題の解き方］

複数人物の写真

　複数人物が写真に写っている場合、主語を表す表現が写真と一致しているか確認しましょう。複数人物が同じ行動をしていて、それを描写している選択肢では、主語を They, People, Customers, Workers などで表していて、動詞部分で共通動作を表しているものが正解の場合が多いです。

1. 🔊)) 07

Ⓐ Ⓑ Ⓒ Ⓓ

2.

Ⓐ Ⓑ Ⓒ Ⓓ

Part 2 Question-Response

Strategy for Part 2 ［応答問題の解き方］

疑問詞で始まる疑問文 ②　Where，Who，When

　疑問文が Where で始まったら、「Where，Where，Where … （どこ？）」のように、頭の中でその疑問詞を繰り返して残しておきます。「場所」を聞かれていることを意識し、選択肢 (A) (B) (C) を聞き終わるまで忘れないように練習してみましょう。

🔊)) 08

3. Mark your answer on your answer sheet.　　Ⓐ Ⓑ Ⓒ

4. Mark your answer on your answer sheet.　　Ⓐ Ⓑ Ⓒ

5. Mark your answer on your answer sheet.　　Ⓐ Ⓑ Ⓒ

6. Mark your answer on your answer sheet.　　Ⓐ Ⓑ Ⓒ

Questions 7-9　　　　　　　　　　　　　　　　　　　　　　　　🔊 09

7. What do the man and the woman do at the museum?
   (A) Manage the art exhibits
   (B) Lead tours
   (C) Collect donations
   (D) Restore paintings

8. What most likely is causing the increase in the museum visitors?
   (A) Free parking
   (B) Extended hours of opening
   (C) A new exhibit
   (D) Painting donations

9. According to the man, what will happen on Tuesday?
   (A) Tickets will be on sale.
   (B) A book signing
   (C) A city official will give a speech.
   (D) An art collector will hold a conference.

Part 4 Talks

Strategy for Part 4 ［説明文問題の解き方］

ガイドツアー

　観光地、美術館、博物館、動物園、工場見学などのツアーガイドによる説明文が頻出問題です。ガイドの自己紹介に始まり、目的地の説明、休憩について、注意事項、帰りの時刻について、と説明文は続きます。

Questions 10-12　　　🔊 10

10. What event is the speaker mainly talking about?

　(A) A sports competition

　(B) First-day opening

　(C) A nutrition workshop

　(D) A community festival

11. What should the guests ensure to participate in the photo competition?

　(A) Look at the animals

　(B) Take photographs and submit them

　(C) Read the contest rules

　(D) Use their camera flash

12. Where can the tourists see the terms of the competition?

　(A) At the zoo's entrance

　(B) At the reception

　(C) In the zoo's official website

　(D) In the animal cages

Part 5 Incomplete Sentences

Strategy for Part 5 ［短文穴埋め問題の解き方］

【語彙問題　語彙フレーズ】

　語彙問題の特徴は、**同じ品詞が選択肢に 4 つ並んでいる**ことです。品詞が同じなので、UNIT 1 で学習した【品詞識別問題】のように、空所およびその前後の品詞を識別するだけでは、答えが導き出せません。解答のポイントは、以下の 3 つです。

　　① 問題文を読み、空所以外の内容を把握すること
　　② 空所と前後の語句が適切に結びつくこと
　　③ 最終的な文の意味を成立させること

「語彙の意味で解くパターン」

　文脈を理解して適切な語を選ぶ、といった基本的な問題が多く出題される傾向にあります。綴りが似ている語彙の意味を混同しないように注意しましょう。

例題 1　The Jaguar, which mounts a hydrogen-fueled engine, is a family car with the -------
to accommodate six people at most.

　　　　(A) effect　　　　　　(B) prevention　　　　　(C) compensation　　　　(D) capacity

解説　まず、空所以外の内容を把握しましょう。「ジャガーは水素エンジンを搭載した家庭車であり、最大で 6 名まで収容できる ------- を持っている」というような内容です。空所後の to accommodate は、直前の名詞を形容詞のように修飾し「収容するための○○」という意味になります。つまり、空所の語彙はその意味とつながりのある名詞でなければなりません。選択肢の意味は、(A)「影響」、(B)「予防」、(C)「補償」、(D)「能力」です。空所の後とつながり、収容人数を適切に説明できるのは (D) です。

* capacity to V「V する能力がある」

参考訳　水素燃料エンジンを搭載した Jaguar は最大で 6 名収容できる一般家庭用の車です。

「フレーズを活用して解くパターン」

　語彙問題にはフレーズ全体が選択肢にある場合と、空所前後にフレーズの一部が記されている場合があります。前後の語句とのつながりや相性を考えましょう。意味的・形式的な結びつきに細心の注意を払い、消去法で解くこともできます。

例題 2　Prices at Burton Hotels are ------- to a temporary change based on decreasing number of visitors due to a recession.

　　　　(A) subject　　　　　(B) plain　　　　　　(C) general　　　　　　(D) public

解説　まず、空所の前後、are ------- to の形を意識しましょう。空所前の Prices at ~「ホテルの料金」
とその後の to a temporary change「一時的な変更に」の関係を説明するフレーズが入ると考えられ
ます。そして、選択肢の意味は、(A)「受ける、さらされる」、(B)「明白な」、(C)「一般的な」、(D)「公
共の」です。前置詞 to とフレーズを成すのは、(A) のみです。また、(A) 以外の選択肢は、「ホテル料
金は」「一時的な変更に」という空所前後の意味とつながりがありません。
* be subject to 名詞「名詞を受ける、名詞を必要とする」
参考訳　不景気による客数減少のせいで、Burton Hotels は料金の一時的な変更を余儀なくされてい
る。

13. ------- priced menus and a family-friendly atmosphere have attracted a majority of tourists.
(A) Provisionally　(B) Thoroughly　(C) Tentatively　(D) Reasonably

14. Before it is fully reserved, visitors planning to participate in a bus tour to see the castle had better ------- right away.
(A) record　(B) register　(C) approve　(D) express

15. A survey shows that travelers have a strong ------- for eating at local restaurants rather than at luxurious ones.
(A) presumption　(B) prevalence　(C) preference　(D) presence

16. The travel agency intends to ------- a new campaign for more reservations of local trips.
(A) implement　(B) retrieve　(C) deposit　(D) conserve

17. With the pandemic, shopping coupons will have their ------- dates extended by a year.
(A) owing　(B) expiry　(C) mature　(D) conditional

18. Due to an unexpected trouble, they had no choice but to ------- the company retreat.
(A) present　(B) propagate　(C) propel　(D) postpone

19. Even during his pleasure trip to London next week, Mr. Simes will have to be ------- checking his inter-office mail from the hotel.
(A) exactly　(B) timely　(C) occasionally　(D) evenly

20. Travelers of the mountain hiking ------- must have their online tickets issued at the gate.

    (A) excursion   (B) reservation   (C) itinerary   (D) exaggeration

21. A ------- in schedule dissatisfied a number of tourists who had looked forward to the local events.

    (A) conservation   (B) consumption   (C) conflict   (D) compartment

Part 6   Text Completion

Strategy for Part 6 ［長文穴埋め問題の解き方］

Part 6 は先に選択肢を見てから文書全体を一気に読んで解答しましょう。TOEIC は 2016 年 5 月に現在の形式となり、Part 6 では空所に入る「文」を選ぶ問題が出題されるようになりました。この「文選択問題」は「文書の文脈を読み取る」ことが必要とされますので、文選択問題は文脈をつかんだ後、4 問の最後に解くことをお勧めします。

Question 22-25 refer to the following e-mail.

To: <multiple addresses>
From: <guardian-aviary@coomail.com>
Subject: Change of Rates

Dear Valued Patrons:

For the last six years, we have charged the same affordable prices for our Big Bird Tours, including visits to the Vulture's Nest, Ostrich Playpen, and our King Penguin and Emu Haven.

We regret that the new government mandate on higher taxes for privately-owned zoos has forced us to raise our prices by 3% ------- April 1. We have made every
                                                     22.

attempt to avoid this price increase. -------, we refuse to compromise the well-being
                                                     23.

of our beloved animals. We ensure that our birds are properly-fed, and well-tended

to by our skilled staff members. -------.
                                          24.

We appreciate your ------- and look forward to continuing serving you.
                               25.

Sincerely,

Bernard Welsh, Owner
Guardian Aviary

22. (A) practical
    (B) critical
    (C) effective
    (D) alternate

23. (A) To an extent
    (B) Therefore
    (C) Accordingly
    (D) However

24. (A) We believe that you will continue to find our zoo most pleasant.
    (B) Our efforts to maintain our pigpen was unsuccessful.
    (C) We hope our competitors will also do a price increase.
    (D) Our place is the best of the best.

25. (A) support
    (B) supporter
    (C) supported
    (D) supportive

Part 7   Single Passages / Multiple Passages

Strategy for Part 7 ［読解問題の解き方］

Part 7「読解問題」54 問の内訳は、まず、2 ～ 4 問の設問がついた「シングル・パッセージ」が10 セット、（設問は 147 番から 175 番まで 29 問）、次に 5 問の設問がついた「ダブル・パッセージ」が 2 セット（176 番～ 185 番まで 10 問）、最後に 5 問の設問がついた「トリプル・パッセージ」が3 セット（186 番～ 200 番まで 15 問）となっています。

Questions 26 to 30 refer to the following website.

http://www.cannesmuseum.com/testimonial

Cannes Museum

Client Testimonial
Please share your thoughts about the quality of our facility and services by submitting your name, e-mail address and review.

Name: Evan White
Email: evwhite@mailxz.com
*this will not be posted with your review

Thank you for the wonderful experience of visiting your museum. I realized that you have paintings by reputable artists that cannot be found in any other museum in the city. The staff are very hospitable, and they ensure that all the works of art are not touched needlessly by the guests—an act of authentic love for the art and history that the museum embodies. The glass showcases were neat and clean, neither overly- nor under-crowded, and I noted that your entrance fee has been retained despite the raise of conservation materials. Your guides were truly knowledgeable of the artworks, sculptures, and provided on point answers to those who had questions. I would gladly bring my family on my next visit and tell them about your outstanding hospitality. I will recommend your museum to my friends so they can also enjoy your superb service!

26. What is true about Cannes Museum?

  (A) It only has common paintings.

  (B) It showcases the works of well-known artists.

  (C) It is the only museum in the city.

  (D) They have impudent staff.

27. Which is NOT true about the staff?

  (A) They are respectful.

  (B) They make sure that guests follow protocols.

  (C) They are concerned about the pieces.

  (D) They are indifferent.

28. What does the customer say about the museum's display?

  (A) They were dirty.

  (B) The spacing among pieces were just right.

  (C) It is crowded.

  (D) It is not appealing.

29. What does the customer imply about the museum's guides?

  (A) They are wealthy.

  (B) They are boring.

  (C) They scold the guests.

  (D) They are well-learned.

30. The word "outstanding" on Paragraph 1, line 9, is closest in meaning to

  (A) Overdue

  (B) Mature

  (C) Memorable

  (D) Impressive

UNIT 3

Business / Technology

Vocabulary Check!

Choose an appropriate translation for the following words.

🔊)) 11

1. preliminary ( )	**2.** boost ( )	**3.** branch ( )
4. community ( )	**5.** drenched ( )	**6.** mutually ( )
7. squeeze ( )	**8.** geographic ( )	**9.** sedentary ( )
10. discrepancy ( )	**11.** initiative ( )	**12.** procedure ( )
13. nocturnal ( )	**14.** subordinate ( )	**15.** eligible ( )

a. 絞る	b. 地理上の	c. 夜行性の	d. 手続き
e. 資格のある	f. もちあげる	g. 枝、支店	h. 相違
i. 座ったままの	j. 主導権	k. 前もっての	l. 部下
m. 相互に	n. 共同体	o. びしょぬれの	

🎧 Listening Section

Part 1　Photographs

Strategy for Part 1 ［写真描写問題の解き方］

室内の写真

　室内の写真で、人物が写っていない場合、写真にあるものが選択肢の主語かどうか確認しましょう。写真にないものが主語である場合はもちろん正解ではありません。

1. 🔊 12

Ⓐ Ⓑ Ⓒ Ⓓ

2.

Ⓐ Ⓑ Ⓒ Ⓓ

Part 2 Question-Response

Strategy for Part 2 ［応答問題の解き方］

疑問詞で始まる疑問文 ③ What, Whose, Why

　Why で始まる疑問文は基本的には「理由」を聞いています。Part 2 では、疑問詞で始まる設問に対して "Yes" や "No" で始まる選択肢はほぼ不正解です。Why に対して単純に Because で始まる選択肢も誤答を誘っている場合が多いので気を付けましょう。

🔊 13

3.	Mark your answer on your answer sheet.	Ⓐ Ⓑ Ⓒ
4.	Mark your answer on your answer sheet.	Ⓐ Ⓑ Ⓒ
5.	Mark your answer on your answer sheet.	Ⓐ Ⓑ Ⓒ
6.	Mark your answer on your answer sheet.	Ⓐ Ⓑ Ⓒ

Questions 7-9   🔊 14

7. According to the man, what was a potential danger to the office employees?

    (A) The shiny floor

    (B) The wet wall

    (C) The drenched floor

    (D) The worn out door

8. According to the woman, what might be the cause of the hazard?

    (A) The people-in-charge forgot to squeeze off the excess water.

    (B) The people responsible were not there.

    (C) The people-in-charge are looking down.

    (D) The people-in-charge overworked.

9. What will the woman do next?

    (A) She will clean the floor.

    (B) She will squeeze off the excess water.

    (C) She will see Theresa after work.

    (D) She will observe Theresa's subordinates at work.

Part 4 Talks

Strategy for Part 4 ［説明文問題の解き方］

スピーチ ①

　研修でのスピーチでは、スピーカーが自分の専門分野について話をする場合と、研修に入る前に研修の目的、社内での問題点などを明らかにしてスタートする場面が多く出題されます。

Questions 10-12　🔊 15

10. Where is the venue of the training?

(A) The north branch

(B) The main branch

(C) The south branch

(D) The tree branch

11. What has the company decided on doing?

(A) Using a bio-scanner system

(B) Using a biology computer

(C) Using an identification system

(D) Using a prometric system

12. How long is the training?

(A) 5 hours

(B) 5 days

(C) 5 weeks

(D) 5 months

Part 5　Incomplete Sentences

Strategy for Part 5 ［短文穴埋め問題の解き方］

【語彙問題　文型】

　「品詞識別問題」や「語彙問題」の基礎となるのは「文型」の知識です。**「文型」とは、動詞の意味や性質に応じて文の要素を整列させる一定の規則**です。

「第1文型　SV」

　主語と動詞のみで意味が成立し、目的語をとらない自動詞が用いられます。前置詞などの付加部*が用いられることが多いです。　*付加部とは、文中で必ずしも必要としない語句を指します。

例文　The shop managers went to the head office to attend a monthly meeting.
　　　（店長たちは、月例会議に出席するために本社へ行った。）

「第2文型　SVC」

　動詞の後に主語の性質や状態を説明する補語があり、「S = C」の関係が成立します。be動詞だけではなく、下記の一般動詞も第2文型を導きます。

　「〜になる」become / get / grow / turn　　　　「〜のようである」seem / look / sound
　「〜の感じがする」feel / smell / taste　　　　「〜ままである」keep / remain / stay

例文　He finally became a manager after years of dedication to the job.
　　　（長年の仕事への献身の結果、彼はマネージャーになった。）

「第3文型　SVO」

　動詞の目的や対象を表す目的語がないと成立しません。目的語は主語の性質や状態を説明しないので、「S = O」の関係にはなりません。

例文　The store manager found errors in a shift roster for next month.
　　　（店長は、翌月の勤務シフト表に間違いを見つけた。）

「第4文型　SVOO」

　動詞の後に2つの目的語（① 間接目的語「〜に」② 直接目的語「〜を」）が入ります。この文型では、目的語の順序は常に「①→②」となります。

例文　The manager sent **the head office a monthly report**.
　　　（マネージャーは、本社に月報を送りました。）

● 第3文型への書き換え

　②直接目的語を動詞の直後におく場合は、①間接目的語の前に前置詞（to / for）を補うことで、第3文型に変わります。前置詞の選択は、その動詞が「移動性（A ⇒ B）」を必須としているかどうかです。例えば、動詞sendの場合、「送り主から受取人への移動」を伴います。なので、第3文型に書き換えるときは、前置詞toが必要になります。

TO タイプ　　give / lend / offer / pay / sell / send / show / teach / tell（移動性がある）
FOR タイプ　　buy / cook / choose / do / find / get / leave / make / order（移動性がない）
書き換え文　The manager sent **a monthly report** to **the head office**.
　　　　　（マネージャーは、月報を本社に送りました。）

「第 5 文型　S V O C」
　動詞の目的や対象となる目的語と、さらにその性質や状態を表す補語が入ります。補語は目的語についての補足説明になるので、「O ＝ C」の関係が成立します。
第 5 文型で使う動詞　find / call / choose / name / think / believe / keep / leave / make
例文　We have been able to keep our company running for a decade.
　　　（私たちは、10 年もこの会社を経営できている。）

例題　The good standing company ------- employees with newborn babies childcare leave.
　　(A) retrieves　　　　(B) offers　　　　　(C) requires　　　　(D) acknowledges
解説　まず、文型を確認します。The good standing company「優良企業」は主語であり、その動詞が空所に入ります。第 4 文型だけが間接目的語の後に直接目的語をそのまま置けるので、employees with newborn babies「新生児をもつ従業員」は間接目的語で、childcare leave「育児休暇」は直接目的語だと推測できます。選択肢の動詞は、(A)「～を引き出す」、(B)「（人）に（物）を与える」、(C)「～を必要とする」、(D)「～を認める」という意味です。その中で、(B) だけが第 4 文型をとる動詞なので、正解となります。
参考訳　その優良企業は、新生児を抱える従業員に育児休暇を与えている。

13. The number of office workers applying for team building classes has ------- increased.
　　(A) sharply　　　(B) sharpen　　　(C) sharpness　　　(D) sharp

14. Mr. White is a -------, flexible staff, making him much in demand.
　　(A) assorted　　　(B) sedentary　　　(C) preliminary　　　(D) versatile

15. For business talks with multinational clients, the company took an ------- as an assistant.
　　(A) interpretation　(B) interpreter　　(C) interpretive　　(D) interpret

16. Mr. Mayor is responsible for ------- the necessity of new purchases of office supplies.
　　(A) assess　　　(B) assessed　　　(C) assessing　　　(D) assessment

17. The managers are looking for ------- methods to motivate employees more than now.

    (A) nocturnal   (B) decided   (C) additional   (D) approximate

18. The release of a new laptop model was put off because a problem ------- during testing.

    (A) modified   (B) emerged   (C) imitated   (D) incorporated

19. Despite its cheap price, the computer is the ------- of many that are more expensive.

    (A) equal   (B) equally   (C) equality   (D) equalize

20. The number of seminar ------- has been boosted this quarter since the fees were discounted.

    (A) participates   (B) participants   (C) participation   (D) participate

21. Creating shift rosters that satisfy all of the employees is a difficult ------- for managers.

    (A) tasks   (B) tasking   (C) tasked   (D) task

Part 6 Text Completion

Strategy for Part 6 ［長文穴埋め問題の解き方］

Part 6 に登場する文書の単語数は大体 100 語前後ですので、それほど長くはありません。しかもその種類は非常に限られています。その中で頻繁に出題されるのは e-mail です。

Question 22-25 refer to the following e-mail.

To: emilytocci@fastmail.com <Ms. Emily Tocci>
From: miller.barbara@richtable.com <Barbara Miller>
Subject: Re Application

Dear Ms. Tocci,

We are delighted to inform you that you have been successful in applying for the position of Information Technology Specialist and will be invited to come to our headquarters for the contract signing and discussion of your ------- on March 15 at
22.
9:30 in the morning.

We would like to request that you bring the remaining requirements you would need to submit, such as your Transcript of Records and a Medical Certificate certifying that you are ------- to work.
23.

Afterwards, we would like to introduce you to Mr. Alan Jackson, the owner and founder of Geronimo Technologies, to formally ------- you, as he would like to
24.
personally discuss the principles of our company.

-------.
25.
We look forward to seeing you soon.

Regards,
Barbara Miller
HR Manager

---

22. (A) employment   (B) working   (C) rules   (D) work gap history

23. (A) unreliable   (B) eligible   (C) reliable   (D) unable

24. (A) complain   (B) acquit   (C) acquaint   (D) observe

25. (A) Kindly reply to acknowledge receipt of this email.
   (B) Don't forget to send your cover letter.
   (C) Don't forget the rescheduled appointment time.
   (D) Kindly receive this email.

Questions 26 to 30 refer to the following article.

Four Seasons Corporation Acquires H. Wells Bistro Group

LOS ANGELES (May 7)—Last month, Four Seasons Corporation (FSC), located in California, announced that it had acquired H. Wells Bistro Group. The largest food corporation in the county said the deal for the H. Wells will help it establish more bases in new areas as part of an initiative to expand, as well as to extend its reach into smaller establishments. H. Wells Bistro Group caters to smaller cities in Los Angeles, such as San Marino and Malibu.

"H. Wells is one of the oldest and most reputable group of small restaurants that unified all bistro owners, building a community of owners that strive for excellence, and we are thrilled to acquire such a fine company, not only to expand in other regions, but to mutually improve the food business in the long run," President Hailee Wells told local reporters at a press conference. "We welcome H. Wells Group's employees to FSC and look forward to working together for the benefit of all." She added that no workers are expected to lose their jobs as a result of the acquisition.

"The H. Wells acquisition is a key step in FSC's strategy to establish our company's goal of empowering small businesses, as well as to be recognized as a leading food and service provider in the United States," Wells said. "Our vision is expanding our geographic reach through partnerships with industry-leading companies."

26. What event had occurred during the previous month?

(A) A restaurant was acquired.

(B) An acquisition took place.

(C) A local hotel merged with a restaurant.

(D) A company was acquitted.

27. Why did Four Seasons Corporation purchase H. Wells Bistro Group?

(A) FSC needs to earn more revenue in Malibu.

(B) FSC wants to broaden its scope across the country.

(C) H. Wells Bistro Group was going bankrupt.

(D) H. Wells needs to extend its reach.

28. What is true about H. Wells Bistro Group?

(A) They are a small company.

(B) They focus on building relationships among bistros.

(C) They host marathons.

(D) They do their best to serve residences.

29. What is NOT true about the acquisition?

(A) H. Wells will work together with FSC.

(B) Some H. Wells employees will be laid off.

(C) FSC embraces the new company and its workers.

(D) FSC will strengthen H. Wells Bistro Group.

30. According to the article, what will FSC likely do in the future?

(A) Reduce staff

(B) Build new restaurants

(C) Work with other companies

(D) Appoint a new president

UNIT 4

Hotel

Vocabulary Check!

Choose an appropriate translation for the following words.

🔊 16

1. gorgeous (　　)　　2. inconvenience (　　)　　3. extension (　　)

4. exquisite (　　)　　5. manor (　　)　　6. buffet (　　)

7. refund (　　)　　8. identification (　　)　　9. temporarily (　　)

10. architect (　　)　　11. registration (　　)　　12. additional (　　)

13. internal (　　)　　14. courier (　　)　　15. affiliated (　　)

a. 延長の、内線の	b. 建築家	c. 内部の	d. 身元証明
e. 追加の	f. 提携の	g. 極上の	h. 荘園
i. ビュッフェの	j. 返金	k. 登録	l. 宅配係
m. 豪華な	n. 不便	o. 一時的に	

🎧 Listening Section

Part 1　Photographs

Strategy for Part 1 ［写真描写問題の解き方］

風景の写真

　風景の写真で、人物が写っていない場合、選択肢の動詞部分が人物のする行動であるかどうか考えてみましょう。人が行う行動であれば、風景写真では表すことができないため、間違いとなります。

1.

🔊 17

Ⓐ Ⓑ Ⓒ Ⓓ

2.

Ⓐ Ⓑ Ⓒ Ⓓ

Part 2 Question-Response

Strategy for Part 2 ［応答問題の解き方］

疑問詞で始まる疑問文 ④ What, How, Which

　How で始まる疑問文は「～どうですか？」の意味だけではなく、そのあとに続く語によって、How many ～, How much ～, How long ～, How far ～ など、数、量、金額、長さ、遠さなどを聞いています。一度マスターすれば、次に出てきた際にイメージしやすいでしょう。

🔊 18

3.　Mark your answer on your answer sheet.　　　Ⓐ Ⓑ Ⓒ

4.　Mark your answer on your answer sheet.　　　Ⓐ Ⓑ Ⓒ

5.　Mark your answer on your answer sheet.　　　Ⓐ Ⓑ Ⓒ

6.　Mark your answer on your answer sheet.　　　Ⓐ Ⓑ Ⓒ

Strategy for Part 3 ［会話問題の解き方］

2 人 × 3 ターンの会話 ①

　Part 3 では登場人物は男女 2 人または 3 人です。会話が男→女→男→女→男→女など、3 ターン以上続く場合もありますが、落ち着いて話の流れについていけば、正解に結びつけることができるでしょう。

Questions 7-9　　　　　　　　　　　　　　　　　　　　　　🔊 19

7. According to the man, what was the problem?

(A) Their order was not hot enough.

(B) Their order was not yet complete.

(C) All their dishes were served.

(D) All their additional dishes were not available.

8. How will the woman fix the issue?

(A) She will make sure the order will be served.

(B) She will use the kitchen.

(C) She will follow the staff into the kitchen.

(D) She will cook the missing salad.

9. What was the alternative suggestion of the woman for the unavailable drink?

(A) Another drink of the same type

(B) A discount

(C) To cancel the order

(D) Another drink not in the menu

Part 4 Talks

Strategy for Part 4 ［説明文問題の解き方］

空港でのアナウンス ①

空港でのアナウンスでは、フライトの搭乗案内、発着時刻に関する話題、天候、その他トラブルによる時刻の変更などが放送されます。

Questions 10-12 🔊 20

10. Where does the announcement most likely take place?
  (A) At a train station
  (B) At a taxi stand
  (C) At a ferry terminal
  (D) At an airport

11. According to the speaker, what has been changed?
  (A) A boarding time
  (B) A refund policy
  (C) A departure gate
  (D) A trip route

12. What does the speaker say the listeners must show?
  (A) An itinerary
  (B) A credit card
  (C) A proof of identity
  (D) A proof of payment

Part 5　Incomplete Sentences

Strategy for Part 5 ［短文穴埋め問題の解き方］

【動詞（時制）問題 ①　態と数】

　動詞（時制）問題では、1 つの動詞の変化形が選択肢に並んでいます。文の意味をとらず、前後の語句から**「態」**を識別し、**「主語動詞の一致」**することで答えられる問題です。

「能動態」

動作主（主語）の行為（動詞）が対象（目的語）に作用する関係を表す文

例文 Buffet lunch at the luxury hotel <u>features</u> a famous pastry chef.

　　（その高級ホテルのビュッフェランチは、ある有名なパティシエを特集している。）

主語：Buffet lunch　　　動詞：features　　　目的語：a famous pastry chef

他動詞 feature が作用する対象・目的となる語があるので、第 3 文型（SVO）の能動態です。

「受動態」

動作を受ける側（目的語）を主語にした「～される」という受身関係を表す文

例文 A famous pastry chef <u>is featured</u> with buffet lunch at the luxury hotel.

　　（ある有名なパティシエは、その高級ホテルのビュッフェランチで特集されている。）

主語：a famous pastry chef　　　動詞：is featured　　　目的語：なし

　能動文の目的語 a famous pastry chef が、受動文で主語になります。そのときに、動詞を**「Be 動詞＋動詞の過去分詞形」**で表します。また、能動文の主語 Buffet lunch は、受動文では前置詞句**「*by（～によって）＋行為者」**で文末へ移動します。ただし、前置詞句は文型を決める構成要素ではないので、第 3 文型の能動文は、主語と動詞の第 1 文型に変わります。

「主語と動詞の一致」

　英語は主語によって適切な動詞の形が変化します。受動態を含め、他の動詞（時制）関連の問題を解くときは「主語の人称、単複」にも注意しましょう。主語が「三人称単数現在の場合の -s」はもちろん大事ですが、次の表現が主語になるときは注意が必要です。

① (Both) A and B ＝動詞は複数形にする（Both you and I *are* …）

② (Either) A or B ＝動詞は「**B**」に一致する（Either you or I *am* …）

③ (Neither) A nor B ＝動詞は「**B**」に一致する（Neither you nor I *am* …）

④ Not only A but also B ＝動詞は「**B**」に一致する（Not only you but also I *am* …）

⑤ A as well as B ＝動詞は「**A**」に一致する（You as well as I *are* …）

例題 Once the computer's virus -------, a lot of information on guests disappeared.

    (A) will be removed   (B) is removing   (C) was removed   (D) removed

解説 接続詞 Once が導く節を確認しましょう。主語 the computer's virus の後に空所があり、単数名詞の主語 virus と一致する動詞が入ると考えられます。ここで、選択肢の動詞 remove「～を取り除く」と主語の関係を考えましょう。空所の直後に目的語がないこと、「ウイルスは取り除かれる側」であることから、答えは受動態だと推測できます。主節 a lot of ～ が過去時制を指しているので、未来形の (A) ではなく、(C) was removed が正解。

参考訳 そのコンピュータのウイルスが取り除かれると、宿泊者の多くの情報が消えていた。

13. All the aspiring service staff for concierge positions ------- to have at least 10 years' experience at foreign affiliated hotels.

    (A) require   (B) is required   (C) has required   (D) requiring

14. The guest demanded that her money be ------- after she had suffered water leakage from the ceiling of her room.

    (A) refunds   (B) refunding   (C) refund   (D) refunded

15. All the service staff ------- to work together to ensure more completed tasks since last week.

    (A) are asked   (B) has been asked (C) has asked   (D) is asking

16. Once the extension line ------- due to the storm, guests could not make any calls.

    (A) was disrupted   (B) was disrupting   (C) disrupted   (D) disrupts

17. The cleaning team suggested that the ventilation fans in men's toilet ------- replaced because of their constant noise.

    (A) was   (B) be   (C) are   (D) were

18. At this time of year, a huge coming-of-age ceremony ------- in Central Plaza Hotel.

    (A) is held   (B) held   (C) is holding   (D) holds

19. Ms. Cooper had dinner in a hotel with her colleagues while her husband ------- in a different hotel with his new clients.

    (A) has dined   (B) dines   (C) will dine   (D) was dining

20. Those who applied for an internal transfer ------- a result of the screening last week with details on the second stage of the selection process.

    (A) were sending

    (B) sent

    (C) were sent

    (D) would send

21. The order that we made for the opening reception has not arrived yet, and the courier tells us that it ------- now and will arrive soon.

    (A) is being delivered

    (B) will deliver

    (C) is delivering

    (D) is delivered

Part 6　Text Completion

Strategy for Part 6 ［長文穴埋め問題の解き方］

　Part 6 でよく登場する文書の種類の１つに「案内」があります。特に TOEIC で出題される案内は、友人などへの個人的なものではなく、主に仕事上、何か伝える必要性のある内容を受け取った人に知らせるものです。

Question 22-25 refer to the following announcement.

Don't feel like coming down to the lobby to join us for breakfast?

As part of our continuous quality service to our guests here in White Flower Hotel, we now introduce our online breakfast ordering system!

First, go to www.whiteflower/breakfast.com.

Next, fill in the ------- information, such as your name, room number, contact
        22.
details.

Your details will only be ------- saved in our system to ensure your privacy.
        23.

You will be directed to the next page which will showcase our menu. Choose the items you wish to avail, and you will see additional options for each meal you select. After specifying your preferences, it will be added to your cart. ------, click
24.
the cart icon, and you will see the summary of the items you picked with the price breakdowns, along with the mode of payment. Once you're set, click the "Order now" button. For the final step, select what time you would like to have your breakfast served straight to your room. ------.
25.

22. (A) helpful   (B) kind   (C) critical   (D) necessary

23. (A) temporarily   (B) eternally   (C) perpetually   (D) primarily

24. (A) finally   (B) next   (C) first   (D) eventually

25. (A) Your food is ready.
(B) Our attendants will serve you your breakfast on the dot.
(C) Don't forget to heat the dishes.
(D) We wish you good luck on your endeavor.

Part 7

Single Passages / Multiple Passages

Strategy for Part 7 ［読解問題の解き方］

　Unit 3 で紹介した、Part 7 のいくつかの設問の種類を意識すると、一見様々なことをたずねているように見える設問のイメージがそれぞれ、はっきりとしてきます。文書のどこにヒントが隠れているか、選択肢は具体的なものか、抽象的なものかなど、様々なことに気づくでしょう。また、Part 7 では「読む力」と「選択肢を選ぶ力」の両方が要求されます。2 つの力をバランスよく鍛えていきましょう。

Questions 26 to 30 refer to the following website.

---

http://whiteorchidmanor.com

White Orchid Manor — Open House

Located at the heart of Ohio in Hillton Cincinatti, the White Orchid Manor is a unique venue for various events such as birthday parties, corporate gatherings, weddings, and a host of other social events. We take great pride in our large and luxurious ballrooms, and we also have small tea rooms inside our hotel, with designated washrooms for each place. Our chefs work with you to perfectly craft your desired menu, and our coordinators will guarantee that your event is superbly organized. Rental pricing is based on the date, type of event, and number of attendees.

You are welcome to tour our facility on April 11 from 10:00 A.M. to 3:00 P.M. Meet with our organizers and culinary staff, and sample items from our exquisite menu. Admission is free, but registration is required. For interested parties, feel free to check our booking page where you can find the available time to visit us. We are offering a 20% discount on any booking made during this open house on April 11.

26. What is being advertised?

    (A) An office rental

    (B) A new hotel

    (C) An event space

    (D) A romantic date

27. What does White Orchid Manor pride itself in?

    (A) Their rich clients

    (B) Newly-renovated ballrooms

    (C) Luxurious bathrooms

    (D) Their elegant ball halls

28. What can visitors try during the Open House?

    (A) A peek inside a party

    (B) Food prepared by the chefs

    (C) A rental room

    (D) Deluxe spaces

29. What will be offered on April 11?

    (A) A discounted reservation rate

    (B) A special concert

    (C) A famous recipe

    (D) A class by a famous chef

30. How long will the event last?

    (A) 3 hours

    (B) 5 hours

    (C) 10 hours

    (D) 5 days

UNIT **5**

Shopping / Purchase

Vocabulary Check!

Choose an appropriate translation for the following words.

🔊 21

1. eagerly ( )	2. merchandise ( )	3. discount ( )
4. slope ( )	5. double ( )	6. warehouse ( )
7. grocery ( )	8. shipment ( )	9. appliance ( )
10. accumulate ( )	11. retire ( )	12. raffle ( )
13. logistics ( )	14. opportunity ( )	15. accessible ( )

a. 利用可能な	b. 流通	c. 機会	d. 熱心に
e. 割引	f. 累積する	g. 出荷	h. 商品
i. 用具、器具	j. 退職する	k. 倉庫	l. 抽選、くじ引き
m. 2倍にする	n. 食料雑貨	o. 坂	

🎧 Listening Section

Part 1 **Photographs**

Strategy for Part 1 ［写真描写問題の解き方］

スーパー、ショップの写真

　スーパーマーケット、人物が何かを購入している写真では、主語には customer, shop clerk, casher, item, merchandise や写真に写っている商品名（books, vegetables 等）が、また、動詞には arrange, purchase, buy などが頻出します。

46

1. 🔊 22

Ⓐ Ⓑ Ⓒ Ⓓ

2.

Ⓐ Ⓑ Ⓒ Ⓓ

Part 2 Question-Response

Strategy for Part 2 ［応答問題の解き方］

一般疑問文 ①　Do you ~ ?, Does he ~ ?

　一般疑問文に対する答え方は、例えば中学校の英語の授業では Do you have a pen? に対して Yes, I do や No, I don't が基本的な答え方だと習いました。しかし、Part 2 においてはそのような基本的な答え方は誤答選択肢として頻出します。引っかからないように注意しましょう。

🔊 23

3. Mark your answer on your answer sheet.		Ⓐ Ⓑ Ⓒ
4. Mark your answer on your answer sheet.		Ⓐ Ⓑ Ⓒ
5. Mark your answer on your answer sheet.		Ⓐ Ⓑ Ⓒ
6. Mark your answer on your answer sheet.		Ⓐ Ⓑ Ⓒ

Strategy for Part 3 ［会話問題の解き方］

3 人の会話 ①

　Part 3 で登場人物が男女 3 人以上の場合、男性または女性のどちらかが 2 人となります。「男性」「女性」という判断だけでは状況を追いかけることが困難な場合もあります。ここでも音声を聞きながら人物の関係や状況を頭の中で想像することが重要になります。

Questions 7-9   🔊 24

7. How does the man describe the location of the thrift shop?

　　(A) It was accessible to his office.

　　(B) It was reachable from the train station.

　　(C) It was far away from the train station.

　　(D) It was near the gas station.

8. Where did the woman's colleague previously work?

　　(A) At a boutique

　　(B) At a lodge

　　(C) At a logistics company

　　(D) At a designer brand company

9. What will the man do next?

　　(A) He will pay by card.

　　(B) He will check the cashier.

　　(C) He will pay for his items.

　　(D) He will come back to the store again.

Part 4　Talks

Strategy for Part 4 ［説明文問題の解き方］

店内のアナウンス

　店内の案内では、季節のセールやイベントなどが紹介されます。イベント、特典の内容や、割引される商品や割引の条件について聞き取りましょう。

Questions 10-12　🔊 25

10. Where is the announcement being made?

(A) At a tech shop

(B) At a clothing shop

(C) At a hardware shop

(D) At a grocery

11. What service is going to be offered?

(A) Cashless payment

(B) Gift wrapping

(C) Good food

(D) Online purchasing

12. Why should the listeners go to the website?

(A) To get vouchers

(B) To gain information

(C) To join a raffle

(D) To get more deals

Part 5　Incomplete Sentences

Strategy for Part 5 ［短文穴埋め問題の解き方］

【動詞（時制）問題②　動詞の時制】

　「態」や「主語と動詞の一致」に加えて、「時制」の正しい理解に基づいて選択肢を判別しなければなりません。ここで、「現在時制・過去時制・未来時制」と「進行形・完了形」を確認しましょう。

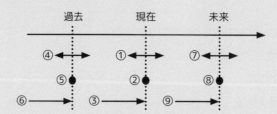

「現在時制のまとめ」

① **現在形（do / does）**

　過去から未来へ一定期間成り立つ状況、日常的な習慣、普遍の原理「〜する、〜である」

② **現在進行形（is / am / are doing）**

　現在している行為「〜している」、状態移行「〜しかけている」、繰り返しの行為「〜ばかりしている」

③ **現在完了形（have / has done）**

　単に現在の状況を述べるのではなく、過去とのつながりを持つ現在の状況を述べます。

　「継続」：ある過去から現在まで続いている動作・状態「ずっと〜している」

　「経験」：これまでの経験が現在とつながっていること「〜したことがある」

　「完了・結果」：これまでに動作が完了したことやその状態「〜してしまった」

「過去時制のまとめ」

④ **過去形（did）**

　（今と関わりのない）過去の行為、過去の習慣、一回限りの出来事「〜した、〜だった」

⑤ **過去進行形（was / were doing）**

　過去にしていた行為「〜していた」、状態移行「〜しかけていた」、繰り返しの行為「〜ばかりしてた」

⑥ **過去完了形（had done）**

　過去のある地点での状況を、「その時まで」のつながりをふまえて述べます。

　「継続」：過去のある時点で、それ以前から継続していたこと「ずっと〜していた」

　「経験」：過去のある時点までに経験したこと「〜したことがあった」

　「完了・結果」：過去のある時点までに動作が完了したことやその状態「〜してしまっていた」

「未来時制のまとめ」

⑦ **未来形（will do / be going to do）**

　will：まだ見ぬ未来の予測「〜だろう」、その場で考えた未来の意志「〜するつもりだ」

　be going to：原因に基づく予測「〜するだろう」、あらかじめ決めていた意図「〜するつもりだ」

⑧ **未来進行形（will be doing）**

未来にしているであろう行為「〜しているだろう」、自然な成り行き「〜しているはずだ」

⑨ **未来完了形（will have done）**

未来のある地点での状況を、「その時まで」のつながりをふまえて述べます。

「継続」：未来のある時点までの今行っている動作の継続「ずっと〜しているだろう」

「経験」：未来のある時点までにしているであろう経験「〜したことになるだろう」

「完了・結果」：未来のある時点で完了している動作とその結果「〜してしまっているだろう」

例題 One of our clerks ------- glad to assist you with your first purchase at this shop now.

    (A) have been   (B) are being   (C) is being   (D) will have been

解説　まず、空所の前後に注目しましょう。One of our clerks「店員の1人」が主語で、後ろに形容詞 glad 〜 があるので、空所には補語をとる動詞が入ります。主語が「A of B」の場合、動詞は「A」の名詞に一致するので、選択肢で単数名詞 One of 〜 と一致しないのは、(A) と (B) です。また、現在完了は now のような「時間軸の一点を指す時の語句」があるときは使用できないので、(D) は不正解。なので、現在形で単数形と一致している (C) is being が正解となります。

＊ be being 形容詞「（いつもではないが）一時的にそのような行動、状態になっている様子」

参考訳　店員の1人は、当店での初めての買い物を手伝うことができてとても喜んでいます。

13. After he ------- the online catalog, David went to the shop to purchase a desk with a 10 percent discount coupon.

    (A) is checking   (B) has checked   (C) checks   (D) had checked

14. Sales at the British tea shop ------- seriously last month because its nearby competitor started to sell British traditional scones.

    (A) suffered   (B) suffers   (C) have suffered   (D) had suffered

15. Once the textbook that he had ordered arrived at him, he found that the cover -------.

    (A) would tear   (B) is tearing   (C) has torn   (D) was torn

16. As a loss leader in April, the managers unanimously ------- kitchen appliances.

    (A) selected   (B) was selected

    (C) is selecting   (D) has been selected

17. To celebrate the opening, the brand ambassador ------- the reception at noon tomorrow.

    (A) is attended   (B) has been attending

    (C) will be attending   (D) will be attended

18. Since the announcement of new smartphone models last week, fans eagerly ------- for the release date.

(A) have been awaiting

(B) was awaiting

(C) awaited

(D) will be awaiting

19. The online store temporarily ------- down for maintenance for three hours this morning.

(A) will be   (B) was   (C) has been   (D) were

20. Before selling used clothes, customers have to declare how many years or times they ------- them so far.

(A) will have worn   (B) wear   (C) have worn   (D) had worn

21. Maria Parker ------- as a store manager for over 10 years by the time she retires.

(A) had served   (B) will have served   (C) has served   (D) has been served

Part 6   Text Completion

Question 22-25 refer to the following announcement.

To our dear shoppers:

It's almost Christmas!
This is a time of giving, and a time to make our loved ones happy with gifts from our hearts!

This December, we have prepared a special treat only for you, our dear shoppers.
For customers who have already ------- our Loyalty Point Card, all points accumulated
                                   22.
from January to December will be doubled by the 31st of December, and you can
use these points as payment for items that you have chosen to buy.

For customers who wish to grab a Loyalty Point Card for themselves starting this month, you still have a ------ to double your points and receive a 10% discount off of
23.
your purchases made on the 31st of December.

Lastly, as our gift to everyone this Christmas season, we will be having a raffle, and you can win as much as $10,000!

For every $250 you ------, you will get one raffle ticket to participate, and the lucky
24.
winners will receive the following prizes:

First Prize: $10,000

Second Prize: A Macbook Pro

Third Prize: An iPhone 12 Pro

Winners will be announced on the first week of January.

------.
25.

Merry Christmas!

22. (A) available   (B) availability   (C) avail   (D) availed

23. (A) change   (B) chance   (C) take   (D) goal

24. (A) spent   (B) spend   (C) spender   (D) expend

25. (A) The prizes are great!
    (B) See you all, and happy shopping!
    (C) We have big sponsors.
    (D) We will ask for your contact details.

Questions 26 to 30 refer to the following e-mail and invoice.

To:	alexa@confettistore.co.nz
From:	quinn_zhie@goomle.co.nz
Date:	September 5
Subject:	Order #45387

Dear Ms. Alexa,

I'm writing to inform you of several problems regarding my most recent order. I have been a loyal buyer from your company for many years, and my previous orders have been delivered with no errors. Therefore, when my latest order arrived, I was very surprised. First, the shipment contained only two packs of T-shirts, which is not the amount listed on the invoice. I saw the note about the long-sleeved shirts, but there was no note about the T-shirts.

On top of that, the price for item #51 is listed in your catalog and on your website as $50 per pack, but that was not what I was charged. Can you please look into this matter and give me a call? You can contact me at +64 09 788 6756.

Thanks in advance,

Quinn Zhie

From:	To:
Confetti Arcade	Quinn Zhie
45 Celedonia Street, Stradmore	Wayward Camp Store
Wellington 6022	89 Juliet Street, Thornland
	Wellington 6011

PAYMENT IS DUE UPON RECEIPT OF INVOICE

Order #45387

Item Number	Item Description	Amount Ordered	Price per Pack	Total Price
32A	T-shirts, white with logo, assorted sizes	3 packs	$125.00	$375
32B* *see note below*	Long-sleeved shirts, white with logo, assorted sizes	3 packs	$175.00	$525
51	Knee-length shorts, limited edition	5 packs	$60.00	$300
118	Black trousers, assorted sizes	2 packs	$200.00	$400
		TOTAL	GST Inclusive	$1,600.00

*We had only one pack of long-sleeved shirts in stock. We included it with this shipment and will send the others in 7-10 business days. There will be no additional shipping charge for these items.

26. Confetti Arcade is most likely what type of business?
   (A) A laundry service
   (B) A clothing company
   (C) A catering firm
   (D) A playground

27. What is indicated about Ms. Zhie?
   (A) She uses several addresses.
   (B) She prefers overnight shipping.
   (C) She has ordered from Confetti Arcade before.
   (D) She is expanding her business.

28. What does Ms. Zhie request?
   (A) An updated catalog
   (B) A new logo design
   (C) A return phone call
   (D) Shipment to a different location

29. According to the invoice, what is true about the long-sleeved shirts?
   (A) They are being billed at a discount.
   (B) They are available in many colors.
   (C) Some items were damaged in the warehouse.
   (D) Some of them will be shipped at a later date.

30. What is one problem that Ms. Zhie identifies?
   (A) Too many trousers were delivered.
   (B) The wrong amount was charged for the shorts.
   (C) The T-shirts do not fit well.
   (D) The logo on the shirts is incorrect.

UNIT 6

Transportation

Vocabulary Check!

Choose an appropriate translation for the following words.

🔊 26

1. compensate ( )　　　2. pedestrian ( )　　　3. feedback ( )

4. complaint ( )　　　5. neighboring ( )　　　6. paralyze ( )

7. passenger ( )　　　8. direction ( )　　　9. malfunction ( )

10. apologize ( )　　11. reconstruction ( )　12. discussion ( )

13. accommodate ( )　14. navigation ( )　　15. construction ( )

---

a. 建設　　　　　b. 意見　　　　　c. 乗客　　　　　d. 話し合い、議論

e. 不具合　　　　f. 苦情　　　　　g. 補償する　　　h. 麻痺させる

i. 収容する　　　j. 謝罪する　　　k. 近隣の　　　　l. 航法

m. 方向　　　　　n. 歩行者　　　　o. 再建築

🎧 Listening Section

Part 1　Photographs

Strategy for Part 1 ［写真描写問題の解き方］

交通の写真

　交通関係の写真では、乗り物の名前に注意して聞きましょう。train, bus, car, taxi, bike, bicycle, track, vehicle などが頻出し、人物は passenger, pedestrian, customer などで表現されることが多いです。

1. 🔊 27

Ⓐ Ⓑ Ⓒ Ⓓ

2.

Ⓐ Ⓑ Ⓒ Ⓓ

Part 2 Question-Response

Strategy for Part 2 ［応答問題の解き方］

一般疑問文 ②　Are you ~ ?,　Is he ~ ?

　Be 動詞で始まる一般疑問文でも、典型的な答え方、例えば Are you a student? に対して Yes, I am や No, I'm not が出てきたら誤答である可能性が高いです。

🔊 28

3. Mark your answer on your answer sheet. 　Ⓐ Ⓑ Ⓒ

4. Mark your answer on your answer sheet. 　Ⓐ Ⓑ Ⓒ

5. Mark your answer on your answer sheet. 　Ⓐ Ⓑ Ⓒ

6. Mark your answer on your answer sheet. 　Ⓐ Ⓑ Ⓒ

Strategy for Part 3 ［会話問題の解き方］

図表を含む問題 ①

　図表を含む問題では、音声が流れる前に設問と図表を見ておく必要があります。しかし図表を見ただけで正解できてしまってはリスニングの問題とならないので、音声と図表の内容の両方から正解を導き出すようになっています。

Questions 7-9 　　　　　　　　　　　　　　　　　　　　　　　　　　🔊 29

Train Guide	
1	Darlington Avenue
2	Lexington Avenue
3	Arlington Avenue
4	Avery Avenue

7. What is the purpose of the man's call?
   (A) To make an appointment
   (B) To request assistance
   (C) To get data
   (D) To talk to Mr. Goldberg

8. Look at the graphic. Which train would the man most likely take?
   (A) Train 1
   (B) Train 2
   (C) Train 3
   (D) Train 4

9. What would the man do after he gets off the train?
   (A) Walk to the office
   (B) Board another train
   (C) Hail a cab
   (D) Block the subway

Part 4 Talks

Strategy for Part 4 ［説明文問題の解き方］

交通情報

　説明文のテーマのうち、交通情報は情報量も多い傾向にあるため、スピーチが早く流れるように聞こえます。聞き取りのポイントは、冒頭から何に関する情報か判断し、現状を捕えます。続いて原因や対処法が流れるのを待ち、今後の指示を待ちましょう。

Questions 10-12   🔊 30

10. What is the main topic of the announcement?

(A) Concert updates

(B) Traffic updates

(C) Road tips

(D) Entertainment news

11. What does the speaker recommend the listeners do?

(A) Check their emails

(B) Avoid the concert site

(C) Check a map

(D) Ignore the traffic

12. What does the speaker say will happen next?

(A) A construction will begin.

(B) A new shopping mall will open.

(C) The Shopping District will be crowded.

(D) A downturn of the economy

Part 5 Incomplete Sentences

Strategy for Part 5 ［短文穴埋め問題の解き方］

【動詞（時制）問題③　分詞・分詞構文】

　動詞問題の選択肢には態や時制に合わせた動詞の活用形だけでなく、「分詞」が含まれていることも多いので動詞と分詞を判別することが必要です。では、分詞を確認していきましょう。

「分詞とは？」

　分詞には「**現在分詞**」と「**過去分詞**」があり、形容詞のように名詞を修飾することができます。分詞の位置に関しては、以下の 2 パターンに分かれます。

①「分詞のみで修飾する場合」＝修飾される名詞の前に置く（**前置修飾**）　※後置修飾も可能。

②「他語句を伴って分詞で名詞を修飾する場合」＝修飾される名詞の後に置く（**後置修飾**）

「現在分詞　V-ing」

　「修飾される名詞」と「分詞」の間に、「**～している・～する**」という能動関係が成立します。その関係は「修飾される名詞＋ V（be 動詞＋ V-ing）」の能動文で表すことができると覚えましょう。

例文 Because of the rising rent, people start to leave urban cities.

　　　（高騰する家賃のせいで、人々は都会を去りはじめている。）

「過去分詞　V-ed　＊不規則活用有り」

　「修飾される名詞」と「分詞」の間に、「**～される・～された**」という受動関係が成立します。その関係は「修飾される名詞＋ be 動詞＋ V-ed)」の受動文で表すことができると覚えましょう。

例文 The flights scheduled for this afternoon were canceled due to the typhoon.

　　　（今日の午後に予定されていた便は、台風のせいで欠航になった。）

「分詞構文」

　「接続詞＋主語＋動詞」を分詞で表し、主節を修飾するときの構造を指します。副詞節のように、補足的な情報を付け加える役割があります。代表的な意味は、「～とき（when）」「～なので（because）」「～ならば（if）」「～だけれども（although）」「～しながら（while）」です。

分詞構文の作り方

① 接続詞とその主語*1 を消す

*1「接続詞のある節の主語＝主節の主語」が同一でない場合は省略はしない。

　　例文　~~Because he~~ had no money, he was not able to use any transportation.

② 動詞を分詞*2・3 に換える

*2「主語と動詞が能動関係」の場合、動詞を「現在分詞」に変換する。

　　現在分詞に換える動詞が「be 動詞」の場合は、「being」または省略する。

　　「主語と動詞が受動の関係」の場合、動詞を「過去分詞」に変換する。

*3 接続詞のある節の時が主節が表す時よりも「前」の場合、having ＋過去分詞にする。

例文　~~Because he~~ had no money, he was not able to use any transportation.

分詞構文　**Having** no money, he was not able to use any transportation.
　　　　（（彼は）お金がなかったので、どの公共交通機関も使えなかった。）

例題 Discovery of a suspicious object on the train left lots of passengers ------- at the platforms.

(A) waits　　　　　(B) waiting　　　　　(C) waited　　　　　(D) having waited

解説　まず、主語と動詞を確認しましょう。主語は Discovery ～「電車内の不審物の発見」で、動詞は過去形 left「～を…の状態にしておいた」。選択肢の (A) waits「現在形」(B) waited「過去形」のように時制を持つ動詞はこれ以上入りません。したがって、空所には時制を持たない分詞が入ることが推測できます。leave は第 5 文型で「目的語＝補語」の状態をつくるので、「乗客＝待つ、待っている」という能動関係を成立させる現在分詞の (B) waiting が正解。(D) は、「having」が時制の差を表してしまうので、時制の差を示す語句がない本文には合いません。

参考訳　電車内の不審物の発見が、多くの乗客をホームに待たせてしまった。

13. A storm ------- by heavy rains has paralyzed the traffic in the northeast part of the city.

(A) is accompanied　　　　　(B) accompanying

(C) to accompany　　　　　(D) accompanied

14. A new sleeper train is sure to get any passenger ------- about its space and design.

(A) exciting　　　　　(B) will be excited

(C) excited　　　　　(D) excites

15. Any student ------- a train pass must show his or her student ID card at a window.

(A) purchasing　　　　　(B) has purchased

(C) purchases　　　　　(D) purchased

16. ------- transfer guide as well as station maps, the app is considered the best navigation.

(A) Having displayed　　　　　(B) Display

(C) Displaying　　　　　(D) Displayed

17. After an accident, train staff must announce the ------- arrival time to passengers.

(A) having expected　　　　　(B) expecting

(C) expected　　　　　(D) expect

18. Reconstruction of Central Station will be completed soon, ------- faster transferring between different lines.

(A) allowing
(B) having allowed
(C) allowed
(D) allows

19. ------- discussion with mayors again and again so far, the station staff is sure to succeed in a stamp rally as an event for children in neighboring towns.

(A) Having had
(B) Having
(C) Has
(D) Had

20. King's Cross Station has been an internationally ------- location because the movie *Harry Potter* was once shot there.

(A) recognizes
(B) recognize
(C) recognizing
(D) recognized

21. ------- the arrival time, we had no choice but to choose a limited express.

(A) Considered
(B) Considering
(C) Had considered
(D) Having been considered

Part 6 Text Completion

Strategy for Part 6 ［長文穴埋め問題の解き方］

Part 6 の設問は「文脈に関係なく解ける設問」と、「文脈に沿って解く設問」の 2 つに大別できます。「文脈に関係なく解ける」問題は空所を含む 1 つの文だけを読めば解けるということで、具体的には「品詞問題」「前置詞の問題」「関係代名詞の問題」などが挙げられます。

Question 22-25 refer to the following announcement.

Cancelled Train

13 January

To all Fairway Subways' valued patrons with tickets assigned departure from Kingston Station: Please be advised that one of our designated trips, which is scheduled to depart at 8:30 A.M. on 15 January, ------- due to thunderstorms and
22.
intermittent weather. Our company has decided to compensate all passengers for the -------. We will refund the amount for the portion of your ticket that was not
23.
consumed, and grant all affected passengers $50 in vouchers to recompense -------
24.
the disruption. Kindly approach our Assistance Kiosk staff and they will gladly accommodate you regarding the said matter. -------.
25.

---

22. (A) was canceled   (B) will be canceled (C) had to cancel   (D) is canceling

23. (A) feedback   (B) time   (C) setback   (D) inconvenience

24. (A) above   (B) around   (C) to   (D) for

25. (A) We hope you enjoyed flying with us.
    (B) The complete amount has been refunded to your account.
    (C) Your complaint will be followed up.
    (D) We thank you for your understanding.

Strategy for Part 7 ［読解問題の解き方］

　Part 7 の設問 176 から設問 185 のダブル・パッセージ型は「難しい」というイメージがありますが、両方の文書からヒントを見つけないと解けない設問は 1 セット 5 問中、1、2 問しか出ません。つまりその他の設問は、どちらか一方の文書からヒントを見つければ解けるでしょう。シングル・パッセージ型と同様に、まずは 2 つの文書を一気に読み、どちらの文書にヒントがあるのかを判断し、解答しましょう。

Questions 26 to 30 refer to the following text-message chain and notice.

Emily Brooke 10:25 A.M.
Good morning Ms. Hague. I would like to give you a heads-up that I might be late to our 11:00 A.M. meeting due to a mechanical malfunction in the train I'm currently boarding.

Dana Hague 10:26 A.M.
Good morning. That's quite unfortunate. What measures are being taken to ensure that passengers can arrive to their destination on time?

Emily Brooke 10:27 A.M.
There was an announcement just now that we would have to alight the current train and walk back to the previous station since it is much nearer than the succeeding one.

Dana Hague 10:28 A.M.
Oh my. That's truly inconvenient!

Emily Brooke 10:29 A.M.
Indeed. I will be boarding the alternative train that departs the earliest, so I believe I will arrive at the office at around 11:10 A.M. I'm truly sorry for the trouble.

Dana Hague 10:30 A.M.
Alright, I got it. We will proceed with the meeting as scheduled and just inform the client that you will be arriving much later for your presentation. Take care!

NORTHEASTERN TRAIN NOTICE

Due to an unexpected engine trouble in one of our units, some of our trains will be delayed. Please refer to this guide to find other routes:

Cancelled Train	Line	Schedule	Other Route	Line	Schedule
A	2	10:20 A.M.	G	4	10:50 A.M.
C	5	10:25 A.M.	B	6	10:55 A.M.
E	3	10:30 A.M.	F	7	10:58 A.M.

We truly apologize for the inconvenience. We will do our best to fix the issue to avoid any further delays in other schedules.

26. Why did Ms. Brooke message Ms. Hague?
    (A) To inform her about heading home from the office
    (B) To mention that she will be heading out of the station
    (C) To give her an advance notice of tardiness
    (D) To tell her that she will make it on time for the meeting

27. What seems to be the problem of the train?
    (A) The mechanic was not functional.
    (B) It needs more passengers to board.
    (C) The announcement speakers were broken.
    (D) There was a problem with the engine.

28. What would Ms. Brooke have to do?
    (A) Complain to the train officers
    (B) Head back to the previous station
    (C) Open the lights in the train carriage
    (D) Walk towards the next station

29. According to the notice, which line will Ms. Brooke be using?
    (A) 4   (B) 5   (C) 6   (D) 7

30. According to the notice, what will the station do next?
    (A) Fix the railroad
    (B) Reschedule some trains
    (C) Give complimentary tickets
    (D) Resolve the mechanical malfunction

UNIT 7

Travel

Vocabulary Check!

Choose an appropriate translation for the following words.

🔊 31

1. destination ( )	**2.** inclement ( )	**3.** locate ( )
4. reservation ( )	**5.** coordinator ( )	**6.** fountain ( )
7. unfortunately ( )	**8.** observe ( )	**9.** unoccupied ( )
10. impeccable ( )	**11.** resemble ( )	**12.** critical ( )
13. skyscraper ( )	**14.** security ( )	**15.** assignment ( )

a. 残念なことに	b. 噴水	c. 摩天楼	d. 重要な、重大な
e. 見つける	f. 観察する	g. 申し分ない	h. 安全、保安
i. 似ている	j. 予約	k. 使用されていない	l. 荒れ模様の
m. 割り当て	n. コーディネーター	o. 目的地	

🎧 Listening Section

Part 1 Photographs

Strategy for Part 1 ［写真描写問題の解き方］

空港の写真

　空港の写真では、airplane, airport, runway, lobby などの単語が出題され、飛行機が離陸しようとしている、滑走路を走っているなどの状態、空港の待合室などの状況も頻出します。

1. 🔊 32

Ⓐ Ⓑ Ⓒ Ⓓ

2.

Ⓐ Ⓑ Ⓒ Ⓓ

Part 2 **Question-Response**

Strategy for Part 2 ［応答問題の解き方］

一般疑問文 ③　Did they ~ ?, Were you ~ ?

　質問に対して Yes, No で答える以外にも、詳細情報についてコメントしたり、会話がスムーズに流れていれば正解です。

🔊 33

3. Mark your answer on your answer sheet.　　　Ⓐ Ⓑ Ⓒ

4. Mark your answer on your answer sheet.　　　Ⓐ Ⓑ Ⓒ

5. Mark your answer on your answer sheet.　　　Ⓐ Ⓑ Ⓒ

6. Mark your answer on your answer sheet.　　　Ⓐ Ⓑ Ⓒ

Part 3   Conversations

Questions 7-9   🔊 34

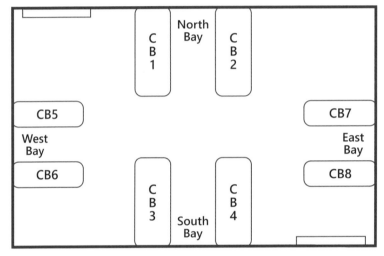

7. What was the problem?

   (A) There was a mix-up of passengers.

   (B) An airplane went missing.

   (C) There was a confusion in the bags.

   (D) Two airplanes lost their baggage.

8. Look at the graphic. Where would the man and the woman get their things?

   (A) West Bay

   (B) South Bay

   (C) East Bay

   (D) North Bay

9. Why was the man worried?

   (A) He couldn't see his bag.

   (B) It will take time for him to find his bag.

   (C) His bag is easy to find.

   (D) His bag was not in the aircraft.

Part 4　Talks

Strategy for Part 4 ［説明文問題の解き方］

空港でのアナウンス ②

　空港でのアナウンスのうち、搭乗案内では、冒頭で目的地が明らかになり、多くは搭乗客への指示（そのままお待ちください、チケットを準備してください、手荷物を確認してください）などで締めくくられます。

Questions 10-12　　　　　　　　　　　　　　　　🔊 35

10. Where does this announcement most likely take place?

(A) At a ferry port

(B) At an airport

(C) At a bus station

(D) At a travel agency

11. According to the speaker, what can the listeners do for free?

(A) Check in extra luggage

(B) Change seat reservations

(C) Check out a baggage

(D) Change flights

12. What does the speaker ask the listeners to do?

(A) Look at their ticket

(B) Change seat assignment

(C) Provide identification

(D) Line up for boarding

Part 5　Incomplete Sentences

Strategy for Part 5 ［短文穴埋め問題の解き方］

【動詞（時制）問題 ④　知覚動詞・使役動詞】

　「知覚動詞」や「使役動詞」のように動詞の中には、特定の形を導くものがあります。空所の前後を確認するだけでなく、そういった動詞が含まれているかも確認しておきましょう。

「知覚動詞」

　以下の知覚動詞はすべて、人間の感覚器官の働きによって行われる動作を示します。

視覚を表す動詞：see / watch / look at / notice / perceive / observe

聴覚を表す動詞：hear / listen (to)　　触覚を表す動詞：feel

嗅覚を表す動詞：smell　　　　　　　　味覚を表す動詞：taste

　これらの動詞は、第 3 文型だけではなく、第 5 文型（O = C）の構造をとることもできます。補語（C）の部分にくる動詞の形は以下の 3 パターン。

① 主語＋動詞＋目的語＋**原形動詞**「O が～するのを V する」

② 主語＋動詞＋目的語＋**現在分詞**「O が～しているのを V する」

③ 主語＋動詞＋目的語＋**過去分詞**「O が～されるのを V する」

①では、目的語の動作の始まりから終わりまでを知覚することを指しますが、②は目的語の動作の一部を知覚することを指します。③は、過去分詞が使われていることから、目的語が何らかの行為を受けている状態を指します。

例文　At baggage claim, travelers **notice** their trunks **opened** for security reasons.

　　（手荷物検査場で、旅行客は保安上の理由で荷物が開けられるのに気づく。）

「使役動詞」

　主語が「目的語に～させる・～してもらう」という意味の動詞です。第 5 文型で「目的語＝補語」の関係を作ります。使役動詞はそれぞれニュアンスが違い、特定の形を補語に取ります。

① **have**「当たり前のことをしてもらう」というニュアンスを含む。

　❶ 主語＋ have ＋目的語（**人**）＋**原形動詞**「S は人に～してもらう」

　❷ 主語＋ have ＋目的語（**物**）＋**過去分詞**「S は物を～してもらう・される」

② **get**「お願いや説得をして、何かをしてもらう」というニュアンスを含む。

　❶ 主語＋ get ＋目的語（**人**）＋ **to 不定詞**「S は人に～してもらう」

　❷ 主語＋ get ＋目的語（**物**）＋**過去分詞**「S は物を～してもらう・される」

③ **let**「したいことを許可して、やらせてあげる」というニュアンスを含む。

　❶ 主語＋ let ＋目的語（**人**）＋**原形動詞**「S は人に～させてあげる」

④ **make**「強制的にさせる」というニュアンスを含む。

　❶ 主語＋ make ＋目的語（**人**）＋**原形動詞**「S は人に～させる」

例文　Since the baggage was beyond a prescribed weight limit, we had to **get** some goods **taken** out of it before tickets were issued.

　　（その荷物が既定の重量制限を超えていたので、発券前に荷物を取り出さなければならなかった。）

例題 The passenger made a complaint about a double-booking, demanding a seat upgrade, and the airline company ended up getting her request -------.
　(A) accept 　　　　(B) accepting 　　　　(C) to accept 　　　　(D)accepted

解説　end up Ving「結局〜する」と使役動詞 get がつながっています。目的語 her request「彼女の要求」は、人以外（もの）だとわかるので、to 不定詞「人に〜させる」という表現は入りません。第 5 文型では、「目的語＝補語」の関係が成立することから、選択肢にある他動詞 accept との関係を考えると、「要求」は「容認される側」なので (D) accepted が正解です。

参考訳　その乗客はダブルブッキングに対して抗議をし、席のアップグレードを要求した。そして、航空会社は結局その要求をのむことになった。

13. To prevent unexpected ignition in an airplane, any passenger is reminded to have his or her lighters ------- before boarding.
　(A) disposed 　　(B) disposing 　　(C) dispose 　　(D) to dispose

14. At baggage claim, the security guard sometimes notices travelers mistakenly ------- up wrong bags that are not tagged with their own baggage number.
　(A) picking 　　(B) picked 　　(C) picks 　　(D) to pick

15. Any passenger has to have his or her luggage ------- via X-rays to prevent terrorism.
　(A) scan 　　(B) to scan 　　(C) scanned 　　(D) scanning

16. After she had found her flight ticket lost, Ms. Scarlet had to stop by the ticket counter to get a new ticket ------- again.
　(A) issuing 　　(B) issue 　　(C) issued 　　(D) to issue

17. Having ------- his name called, the passenger failed to check in twenty-five minutes before scheduled departure time.
　(A) done 　　(B) had 　　(C) been 　　(D) let

18. One of the duties of flight attendants is to get all of the passengers ------- in the arrival card before landing.
　(A) fills 　　(B) filled 　　(C) to fill 　　(D) filling

19. For more smooth security screening procedures, please remember not to have all metal items including jewelries and accessories ------- in your carry-on luggage.
　(A) placed 　　(B) to place 　　(C) places 　　(D) place

20. Despite several attempts to have his fingerprints -------, Mr. Owens failed it due to a wound with stitches on his thumb.

(A) authorizing   (B) authorize   (C) to authorize   (D) authorized

21. Since Ms. Norris had located three grams of backup lithium batteries in her checked baggage, the airline had to ------- them disposed against her will.

(A) put   (B) do   (C) have   (D) let

Part 6 **Text Completion**

Strategy for Part 6 ［長文穴埋め問題の解き方］

　Unit 6 で紹介した、Part 6 の 2 種類の設問タイプのうちの「文脈に沿って解く問題」を解くには、空所が入っている文だけではなく、その前後の文を読む必要があります。具体的には「文と文をつなぐ語句を選ぶ問題」「動詞の形を選ぶ問題」「語彙を選ぶ問題」などが挙げられます。

Question 22-25 refer to the following e-mail.

To: All New Flight Attendants
From: Ahmed Bahar
Date: Friday, July 16
Subject: Re-training

Dear all,

This is a reminder that we will be having a re-training for our Standard Operating Procedures for Emergency Situations. It was brought to my attention that the previous training showed that majority were not able to live up to our company's standards for emergency response, especially under time constraints. -------, I would
22.
personally be present during the training to observe, and I expect all employees to be inside Training Room 5 on or before 8:00A.M. Tardiness will not be -------.
23.

I also want to ------- the fact that this is a highly critical part of our work as stewards.
24.
Our passengers' safety will always be of the highest priority, so -------.
25.

Ahmed Bahar
Chief Operating Officer

---

22. (A) Therefore   (B) Under no circumstances

    (C) Somehow   (D) Fortunately

23. (A) tolerant   (B) tolerate   (C) tolerated   (D) tolerating

24. (A) hide   (B) stress   (C) importance   (D) forget

25. (A) I hope everyone will come.

    (B) please keep your smartphones on silent mode.

    (C) don't forget to bring your safety gear.

    (D) please bear this in mind at all times.

Part 7 Single Passages / Multiple Passages

Strategy for Part 7 ［読解問題の解き方］

　Part 7 の設問 186 から設問 200 までは、トリプル・パッセージ型です。3 つの文書を読んで解答する設問が 5 問ずつ 3 セット、15 問出題されます。

Questions 26 to 30 refer to the following text message, article and website.

From: Daniel Rondeau [8:03 A.M.]

To: Friedrich Hayes <029 2021 9876>

Hi Friedrich. I'm with the electrical contractors at the former Pathways station now. The electrical system is in way worse shape than we presumed it would be. The rewiring and upgrades would cost us more since we are considering both long-term efficiency and aesthetic of the interior design. I'll send over the estimate as soon as I receive it. Hope we can carry out the work completely in time for the June opening.

New Airport to Open in Virginia

PRIMLAND (18 May)—The Pathways Airport is scheduled to open on 25 June. The building was once a busy train station that was designed by Bernard Jones over 50 years ago.

For almost 20 years, the building had been left unoccupied. It was purchased a year ago by the local government of Primland. According to the project coordinator, Daniel Rondeau, the old building required extensive renovation not only to turn it into an airport but also to update the electrical, plumbing, and heating systems.

The airport is set to have 6 major runways, vast waiting and boarding areas, offices, cafes, shops, and many more facilities that can accommodate almost the same amount of passengers as the airport at the city of Richmond.

In the near future, the mayor of Primland, Mr. Leonard Smith, plans to expand the airport further.

For more information, visit www.pathwaysairport.gov.co

Janna's Blog – Travel and More

Hi everyone, it's Janna here again!
The new airport piqued my interest since I myself had been born and raised in Virginia, and the Pathways Airport was definitely a sight to see in itself. As a traveler and plane enthusiast myself, I was pleasantly surprised to find that it had such up-to-date facilities. The waiting area seats were comfortable—enough to make you fall asleep with the lightly-cushioned seats! You'll have to be careful not to fall asleep while waiting to board your flight though. On top of that, the interior designing was impeccable. It had a minimalist feel to it, and that's what most travelers would find comforting after a long plane ride. And speaking of planes, I was baffled at the sight of the runways! I heard it was expansive, but reality exceeded expectations.

Well, I better allow everyone to see for themselves what this newly-renovated airport has to offer. I'd like to tell you more, but I might spoil your experience.

26. Why did Mr. Rondeau send the text message?

(A) To explain why a project's cost will increase

(B) To request assistance in fixing electrical issues

(C) To warn about the inefficiency of the contractors

(D) To appraise the finished renovation

27. Where was Mr. Rondeau when he sent the message?

(A) At the former airport

(B) Along the path

(C) At the proposed airport site

(D) In the electrical contractor's office

28. What does the article suggest about the new airport?

(A) It will be preserve the integrity of the station.

(B) It will be sold by the government.

(C) It will be at par with the city airport.

(D) It will be inexpensive to renovate.

29. What does the article say about the Pathways Station?

(A) It has been abandoned for years.

(B) It is one of the oldest stations in Virginia.

(C) It has been bought by a private company.

(D) It was designed a century ago.

30. What is suggested in Janna's Blog?

(A) The waiting area was too cold.

(B) The design of the place was of high standard.

(C) It had minimal facilities.

(D) The plane tickets were expensive.

Housing

Vocabulary Check!

Choose an appropriate translation for the following words.

🔊 36

1. countertop ( )	2. analysis ( )	3. cafeteria ( )
4. allocate ( )	5. prototype ( )	6. dormitory ( )
7. residence ( )	8. approval ( )	9. removal ( )
10. curtain ( )	11. expense ( )	12. maintenance ( )
13. participant ( )	14. evacuation ( )	15. botanical ( )

a. 試作品	b. カーテン	c. 避難	d. 支出
e. 維持	f. 参加者	g. 寮	h. 植物の
i. 食堂	j. 承認	k. 除去	l. 割り当てる
m. 住居	n. テーブル	o. 分析	

🎧 Listening Section

Part 1   Photographs

Strategy for Part 1 [写真描写問題の解き方]

住居の写真

　住居の写真では、室内の様子を表したもの、一軒の家にフォーカスをあてたもの、また住宅が立ち並んでいる様子、街並みなどの様々な視点からの写真が出題されます。

1. 🔊 37

Ⓐ Ⓑ Ⓒ Ⓓ

2.

Ⓐ Ⓑ Ⓒ Ⓓ

Part 2 Question-Response

Strategy for Part 2 ［応答問題の解き方］

依頼・許可・提案・勧誘 ①

　Can you ~ ?, May I ~ ? で始まる表現は直訳すると、「~できますか」「~してもいいですか」ですが、単純に相手ができるかどうか、自分がしても良いかを答える選択肢だけが正解ではなく、「~していただけますか」「~をしようと思っています」などのニュアンスで、「依頼」や「許可」を表しています。会話の流れがナチュラルなものを選びましょう。

🔊 38

3. Mark your answer on your answer sheet.   Ⓐ Ⓑ Ⓒ

4. Mark your answer on your answer sheet.   Ⓐ Ⓑ Ⓒ

5. Mark your answer on your answer sheet.   Ⓐ Ⓑ Ⓒ

6. Mark your answer on your answer sheet.   Ⓐ Ⓑ Ⓒ

Strategy for Part 3 ［会話問題の解き方］

2 人の会話問題 ②

　Part 3 で、設問を先に読んでおくことで、ポイントを絞って聞くことができるだけではなく、会話を聞く前に内容を知ることができます。設問の疑問詞と主語のほかの部分にも注意を払うと、音声が流れる前に「男性」が「何か」を「した」（例：電話をした）。もしくは「女性」は「何かをする」と「言っている」などの情報を得ることができるでしょう。

Questions 7-9　　　　　　　　　　　　　　　　　　　　　🔊 39

7. Who is Mr. Park?

    (A) A client

    (B) An assistant

    (C) A homeowners' president

    (D) A construction worker

8. Why did Mr. Park call?

    (A) To request a faster renovation

    (B) To buy counterfeit top

    (C) To install an application software

    (D) To report an error

9. What does the woman say she will do?

    (A) Order extra supplies

    (B) Check the countertop

    (C) Request for an alternative material

    (D) Replace the countertop herself

Part 4 Talks

Questions 10-12 　　　　　　　　　　　　　　　　　🔊 40

10. Which department does the speaker most likely work in?

(A) Marketing

(B) New Product Management

(C) Product Development

(D) At a travel agency

11. Why does the speaker want to meet with the listener?

(A) To assign work

(B) To request for prototypes

(C) To discuss a project

(D) To check the expenses

12. Where is the speaker's office?

(A) Across from the kitchen

(B) Beside the kitchen

(C) Far from the kitchen

(D) Right outside the kitchen

Part 5 Incomplete Sentences

Strategy for Part 5 ［短文穴埋め問題の解き方］

【文法問題 ①　接続詞と接続副詞】

　接続詞や接続副詞が選択肢に並んでいるので、問題の識別は比較的簡単です。文の意味を把握しつつ、空所の後ろにどのような構造があるかを判断する必要があります。

「文法用語のおさらい」

　接続詞と接続副詞を学習するうえで、以下の文法用語を理解しなければなりません。

① 「**語**」：単語１つ１つのことを指す

② 「**句**」：２つ以上の「語」から成り、意味をもつかたまりを指す

③ 「**節**」：２つ以上の「語」から成り、主語（S）と動詞（V）をもっている形

「接続詞」

❶ 等位接続詞：「語と語」「句と句」「節と節」のように、対等（同等）な役割を結びます。and / but / or / for / nor / so などが代表的な等位接続詞です。

「語と語」　Each room of this accommodation is furnished with a desk and a bed.
（この寮の各部屋には、学習机とベッドが備え付けられている。）

「句と句」　The inspector recommended cleaning the sewage pipe or replacing it.
（検査官は、下水道管を掃除する、または取り替えることを勧めた。）

「節と節」　The company received many complaints but they did not make any apologies.
（その会社は、多くの苦情が来たが謝罪をしなかった。）

❷ 従属接続詞：「節と節」を結び、主要な内容（主節）とそれに付随する内容（従属節）の関係が成立します。

「節と節」　Remodeling the interior was an urgent task because the wall was peeling off.
（壁が剥がれ落ちていたので、内装の改装は急務であった。）

主節は、主語 Remodeling the interior、動詞 was、補語 an urgent task から成る第２文型です。the wall（主語）と was（peeling...）（動詞）を含む節は、従属接続詞 because によって導かれた「理由」を表す従属節です。

「接続副詞」

　接続詞と似たような意味を持つため、誤って覚えてしまうことが多いです。however / therefore / otherwise / furthermore などは副詞なので、上記の接続詞のように「節と節」を結ぶことはできません。

（誤）The wall was peeling off, therefore, remodeling the interior was an urgent task.

（正）The wall was peeling off. Therefore, remodeling the interior was an urgent task.

　誤文は、「したがって」の意味を持つ接続副詞 therefore が、接続詞のように節（the wall was ...）と節（remodeling the interior was ...）をつないでしまっているので、非文法的です。正しい文のように、前の文をピリオドで完結させ、接続副詞を置かなければなりません。しかし、次の文のようにセミコロン（；）を用いることで、接続詞のように「節と節」をつなぐことができます。

例文 The wall was peeling off; **therefore**, remodeling the interior was an urgent task.

例題 ------- the schedule says that the reconstruction of a city hall will be completed next month, it must be delayed because of the recent adverse weather.

(A) Until　　　　　(B) Once　　　　　(C) Unless　　　　　(D) Although

解説　カンマ前の内容は「予定では市役所の改築は来月に終わることになっている」です。後半にある it は、動詞 must be delayed から「遅れる、遅延されるもの」とわかるので「reconstruction」を指すと推測できます。よって、意味は「最近の悪天候のせいで改築は遅れるに違いない」となります。カンマの前後に「節（文）と節（文）」があることから、空所には接続詞が入ります。意味を考えると、前半部分の内容に対して、後半部分は予定通りにいかない旨が書かれているので、「譲歩（〜だけれども）」が適切。したがって、(D) Although が正解。その他の選択詞も接続詞ですが、(A) Until「〜までずっと」、(B) Once「一度〜すると」、(C) Unless「〜しない限り」はどれも文意に一致しません。

参考訳　予定では市役所の改築は来月に終わることになっているが、最近の悪天候のせいで改築は遅れるに違いない。

13. A decision on which dormitory to live in will be made ------- she has checked all the equipment available.

(A) thus　　　　(B) despite　　　　(C) right away　　　　(D) as soon as

14. ------- the construction begins, noise is expected to distract residents during the day.

(A) Once　　　　(B) But　　　　(C) In spite of　　　　(D) Promptly

15. Purchase procedure will proceed ------- the purchaser's home loan is approved.

(A) unless　　　　(B) moreover　　　　(C) only if　　　　(D) otherwise

16. All the workers at this construction site have attended an evacuation drill at least once; ------- they would not be working here.

(A) nevertheless　　(B) however　　　　(C) otherwise　　　　(D) still

17. Residents will be allocated a bicycle parking lot ------- they have registered.

(A) unless　　　　(B) though　　　　(C) only if　　　　(D) yet

18. The new plant built in Singapore uses the latest technology ------- eco materials.

    (A) and   (B) however   (C) furthermore   (D) so

19. Those having paid deposits are soon given a special identification number to enter the residence; -------, none of us has been notified of the number yet.

    (A) despite   (B) nonetheless   (C) thus   (D) because

20. University entry has been strictly restricted to those with ------- the approval from the school or urgent business on campus.

    (A) if   (B) either   (C) both   (D) every

21. ------- a lease agreement has been renewed, you are entitled to live here for another two years.

    (A) Since   (B) Although   (C) Thus   (D) Before

Part 6 **Text Completion**

Strategy for Part 6 ［長文穴埋め問題の解き方］

  Unit 6 で紹介した、Part 6 の「文脈に関係なく解ける設問」を解く際は、ある程度の文法力があれば、空所を含む文の前後を読み直さなくても、時間をかけずに解答できます。もし残り時間が少なく、文書をすべて読むことができない場合でも、時間をかけずに解答できる問題を選んで解くことも頭に入れておきましょう。

Question 22-25 refer to the following e-mail.

To: Lan Chen <lchen@smartcomm.org>
From: Andrew Flores <aflores@wellman.org>
Date: April 10
Subject: April 5 Workshops

Dear Mr. Shan,

I am writing to share our ------ for the workshops Ms. Huy Yin delivered at our
22.
corporate headquarters on April 5. Some employees ------ concern regarding the
23.
usefulness of improvisation training in a business setting. As you may know,
competition among construction firms are strong and our sales employees
benefitted very much from scenario analysis and simulation. These same
employees participated fully throughout the day and even inquired about the
possibility of a follow-up session.

We asked our participants to complete our company's evaluation form ------ to
24.
better gauge the effectiveness of the workshops. Results were mainly positive with
90 percent of participants saying their communication skills are more established
now. ------. Please let me know if you would like to discuss the workshops in more
25.
detail.

Best Regards,
Andrew Flores

22. (A) appreciate   (B) appreciative   (C) appreciated   (D) appreciation

23. (A) express   (B) are expressing
(C) had expressed   (D) were to be expressed

24. (A) afterward   (B) often   (C) since   (D) moreover

25. (A) The workshop will be rescheduled next month.
(B) A number of participants said they would have liked more practice.
(C) An additional workshop for teams will be occasionally offered.
(D) We will provide an invoice requesting for your payment.

Questions 26 to 30 refer to the following form.

Work Agreement

Johnson-Brown Landscapers
Email: info@johnsonbrown.com
Website: www.johnsonbrown-landscape.com
Phone: 217- 879-0111

Customer name:	Elizabeth Wellington
Customer phone number:	215-266-2011
Work site:	10 Burgundy Street, Oregon OR
Type of project:	Home garden
Project date:	April 5
Arrival time:	9:00 A.M.
Estimated time of completion:	12:00 Noon

Service	Price
Monthly lawn maintenance (April):	$39.95
Fertilization of garden soil:	$150.00
Delivery and planting of flowers:	$495.00
Project total:	$684.95
Deposit (Paid, April 1):	$200.00
Balance due upon completion:	$484.95

26. What is indicated about the project?

(A) It will begin in the afternoon.

(B) It has been paid in full.

(C) It requires removal of plants.

(D) It includes a regular service.

27. Where will the work take place?

(A) At a flower shop

(B) At a park

(C) At Ms. Wellington's residence

(D) At the offices of Johnson-Brown Landscapers

28. How much was the amount paid before the project?

(A) $39.95

(B) $150.00

(C) $200.00

(D) $495.00

29. At what time of the day will the project be conducted?

(A) At dawn

(B) Late morning

(C) In the afternoon

(D) In the night

30. What amount will Johnson-Brown Landscapers receive on April 5?

(A) $200.00

(B) $484.95

(C) $495.00

(D) $684.95

Entertainment

Vocabulary Check!

Choose an appropriate translation for the following words.

🔊 41

1. encounter ( )　　2. versatile ( )　　3. temperature ( )

4. whistle ( )　　5. convenient ( )　　6. actor ( )

7. celebration ( )　　8. embarrassing ( )　　9. succulent ( )

10. compensation ( )　11. conflict ( )　　12. repertoire ( )

13. subscription ( )　14. annual ( )　　15. volatile ( )

a. レパートリー	b. 年次の	c. 衝突	d. 万能の
e. 恥ずかしい	f. 水気の多い	g. 口笛	h. 定期購読
i. 報酬	j. 俳優	k. 気まぐれな	l. 便利な
m. 気温	n. 祝典	o. 直面する	

🎧 Listening Section

Part 1　Photographs

Strategy for Part 1 ［写真描写問題の解き方］

娯楽の写真

　娯楽の写真では、人物1人がその娯楽を楽しんでいる様子や、複数人物が同じ動作をしている様子、観客が何かを見ている様子が描写されている写真が多く出題されます。

1. 42

Ⓐ Ⓑ Ⓒ Ⓓ

2.

Ⓐ Ⓑ Ⓒ Ⓓ

Part 2 **Question-Response**

Strategy for Part 2 ［応答問題の解き方］

依頼・許可・提案・勧誘 ②　Why don't you ~ ?

　Why don't you ~ ? で始まる表現は直訳すると「どうして～しないの？」ですが、要するに「してもよいのではないですか？（どうしていけないのか？）」のニュアンスで、「提案」や「勧誘」を表しています。

🔊 43

3. Mark your answer on your answer sheet. 　Ⓐ Ⓑ Ⓒ

4. Mark your answer on your answer sheet. 　Ⓐ Ⓑ Ⓒ

5. Mark your answer on your answer sheet. 　Ⓐ Ⓑ Ⓒ

6. Mark your answer on your answer sheet. 　Ⓐ Ⓑ Ⓒ

Part 3 Conversations

Questions 7-9 　　🔊 44

7. What are the speakers mainly talking about?

   (A) A holiday event

   (B) A company marathon

   (C) A cultural celebration

   (D) A trial show

8. What does Megumi offer to do tomorrow?

   (A) Persuade colleagues to join the marathon

   (B) Speak with co-workers

   (C) Finalize the cultural festival

   (D) Invite her friends to the parade

9. What does the project need?

   (A) Cooperators

   (B) Collaborators

   (C) Organizers

   (D) Operators

Part 4 Talks

Questions 10-12   🔊 45

10. What is the purpose of the speaker's call?

(A) To invite guests to the lobby

(B) To confirm a band's onboarding

(C) To request a performance

(D) To fire performers

11. What did the speaker say their company is looking for?

(A) Volatile performers

(B) Adaptable performers

(C) Traditional performers

(D) Additional performers

12. What will the speaker do next?

(A) Meet up with the band

(B) Compensate the band

(C) Sign up as a band member

(D) Agree to all the band's terms

Part 5　Incomplete Sentences

Strategy for Part 5 ［短文穴埋め問題の解き方］

【文法問題 ②　接続詞と前置詞】

　前置詞が接続詞、接続副詞とともに選択肢に並ぶ問題は Part 5 で多く出題されます。前置詞は、時、場所、手段、方向、所有など様々な意味を補足的に表します。ここでは、前置詞が導く構造と前置詞の頻出パターンを学習していきましょう。

「接続詞、接続副詞、前置詞の見分け方」

「接続詞」：　① 等位接続詞の前後には「語と語」、「句と句」、「節と節」が等しく並ぶ。

　　　　　　② 従属接続詞の前後には「節（従属節）」と「節（主節）」がある。

「接続副詞」：「節と節」を結ぶことはできないため、「S + V」は一組だけ。

「前置詞」：　後ろに続くのは、「**名詞**」または名詞のはたらきをする「**名詞相当句**」のみ。

「接続詞と前置詞のよくある間違い」

　「前置詞・接続詞問題」は品詞の見極めができれば解ける問題ですが、同時に品詞を誤りやすい問題でもあります。上記の見分け方とともに、以下の語句を見直しておきましょう。

① 「～にも関わらず」

　【接続詞】although / (even) though　【前置詞】despite / in spite of

② 「～のあいだ」

　【接続詞】while　【前置詞】during

③ 「～なので、～のせいで」

　【接続詞】because / since / as　【前置詞】because of / due to / owing to

④ 「～でない限り、～なしでは」

　【接続詞】unless　【前置詞】without

「相関語句」

　接続語句と組み合わさっている「**相関語句（相関接続詞）**」は、Part 5 では「決まり文句」として出題されています。空所前後に、「相関語句」の一部があるかどうかを確認しましょう。

① both A and B「A と B どちらも」

② either A or B「A か B のどちらか」

③ neither A nor B「A も B も～ない」

④ not only A but (also) B「A だけでなく B もまた」

⑤ A as well as B「B と同様に A も」

⑥ not A but B「A ではなく B」

例題 Due to poor weather, the next ferry service to Southern Island will be suspended ------- 3 o'clock.

(A) by　　　　　　(B) during　　　　　(C) next to　　　　(D) until

解説 選択肢がすべて前置詞なので、内容を確認しましょう。Due to は原因を表すので「悪天候が原因で」の意味になります。the next ferry service (S) will be (V) からなる主節は「次のフェリーが延期される」ことを表しています。動詞 suspend「延期する」から考えると、空所には「〜までずっと」という継続の前置詞が入ると推測できるので、(D) until を選びます。(A) by「〜までに（期限）」、(B) during「〜の間」、(C) next to「〜のとなりに」なので、いずれも意味が合いません。

参考訳 悪天候のせいで、サウザンアイランド行きの次のフェリーは 3 時まで延期になるだろう。

13. The museum will be closed for renovation and will open again ------- the end of July.

(A) on　　　　　　(B) for　　　　　　(C) at　　　　　　(D) to

14. A roller coaster at Central Theme Park has been ------- maintenance since yesterday.

(A) in　　　　　　(B) under　　　　　(C) on　　　　　　(D) by

15. All visitors to the pool now have to check their temperature ------- entering the facility.

(A) prior to

(B) in response to

(C) for the sake of

(D) in order to

16. Workshop participants were asked to put the questionnaire in the box ------- the door when leaving the room.

(A) to

(B) beside

(C) besides

(D) instead of

17. ------- its high admission fee, the flower garden is full of tourists throughout the year.

(A) Even though

(B) Because

(C) In spite of

(D) In terms of

18. Local residents of the town will receive complimentary tickets ------- annual music concerts.
    (A) upon
    (B) by
    (C) at
    (D) for

19. Those invited to the buffet party may hang their coats and jackets in the closet ------- the reception desk.
    (A) between
    (B) into
    (C) near
    (D) until

20. The city has been known for its biggest Ferris wheel ------- a botanical garden featured with unique African succulent plants.
    (A) in spite of
    (B) as well as
    (C) moreover
    (D) in addition

21. Those who have signed up for the subscription will receive a book coupon for online bookstore which goes ------- effect on April 1st.
    (A) in
    (B) into
    (C) for
    (D) from

Part 6 Text Completion

Strategy for Part 6 ［長文穴埋め問題の解き方］

　Part 6 の「文脈に沿って解く設問」の1つ、語彙問題では、選択肢はすべて同じ品詞であり、文法の知識のみでは正解することができません。この際、選択肢にかなり難しい単語が入っていることがありますが、誤答選択肢である可能性が高いため、不用意に意味のわからない単語を含む選択肢を正解に選ばないようにしましょう。

Question 22-25 refer to the following announcement.

The Oklahoma Opera House website is currently ------- because of maintenance.
22.
The updated site can be accessed after midnight tonight. ------- providing
23.
enhanced security to protect your information, the online checkout for tickets will
include an interactive hall seating placements to make reserving from our Opera
House easier than ever. ------- includes a more user-friendly interface. -------. The
24.   **25.**
improvements should provide smoother transactions in the future.

22. (A) ready　　　(B) unavailable　　(C) started　　　(D) complicated

23. (A) Even though　(B) Compared with　(C) In addition to　(D) Even if

24. (A) This　　　　(B) Any　　　　　(C) You　　　　　(D) Mine

25. (A) We are very sorry for the sudden announcement of our closure.
　　(B) A website developer is currently having trouble reopening our site.
　　(C) Unfortunately, we cannot accommodate all reservations anymore.
　　(D) We would like to thank you for your patience during this time.

Questions 26 to 30 refer to the following text-message chain.

Delaney Crow 8:34 A.M.

Are you here yet? We're expected to start the dress rehearsal at 9:15.

Chris Hemming 8:40 A.M.

No way! I thought I heard the director say 9:50! Good thing I'm already on the bus and will be able to get there in 15 minutes.

Delaney Crow 8:42 A.M.

That's good news! I thought I would have to start without my leading actor on stage. That would be too embarrassing for me! Take care and I'll see you.

26. What trouble did Ms. Crow encounter?

(A) Her co-actor is missing.

(B) Her rehearsal was too early.

(C) Her co-actor quit his part.

(D) Her co-actor was skipping rehearsal.

27. What event will be taking place?

(A) A gala show

(B) The final practice before the show

(C) The wearing of dresses

(D) A typical rehearsal

28. At 8:40 A.M., what does Mr. Hemming most likely mean when he writes, "No way"?

(A) He doesn't want to attend.

(B) He is surprised at how early he is.

(C) He realized he made a mistake.

(D) He doesn't believe Ms. Crow.

29. In Delaney Crow's message at 8:42, the word "leading" has the closest meaning to

(A) most important

(B) directing

(C) being in charge

(D) moving forward

30. What is implied about Delaney Crow?

(A) She is the leading lady.

(B) She is the director.

(C) She is in charge of props.

(D) She is a backstage runner.

Hobby

Vocabulary Check!

Choose an appropriate translation for the following words. 🔊 46

1. gratitude ( )	**2.** prioritize ( )	**3.** endurance ( )
4. renowned ( )	**5.** reserve ( )	**6.** urgent ( )
7. reasonable ( )	**8.** revolving ( )	**9.** harvest ( )
10. inquiry ( )	**11.** pedestal ( )	**12.** hazardous ( )
13. amusement ( )	**14.** solicit ( )	**15.** imperative ( )

a. 忍耐力	b. 懇願する	c. 台座	d. 回転する
e. 緊急の	f. 重要な	g. 手ごろな	h. 娯楽の
i. 優先する	j. 問い合わせ	k. 予約する	l. 収穫する
m. 危険な	n. 感謝	o. 有名な	

🎧 Listening Section

Part 1 Photographs

Strategy for Part 1 ［写真描写問題の解き方］

趣味、芸術の写真

　趣味、芸術の写真では、人物がスポーツ、芸術鑑賞、旅行など、様々な動作を行っている場面や、絵画、芸術作品、試合会場、旅行先の風景そのものの写真であることが考えられます。

1. 🔊 47

Ⓐ Ⓑ Ⓒ Ⓓ

2.

Ⓐ Ⓑ Ⓒ Ⓓ

Part 2 **Question-Response**

Strategy for Part 2 ［応答問題の解き方］

依頼・許可・提案・勧誘 ③ Would you mind if ~ ?

　Would you mind if ~ ? で始まる表現は、直訳すると「もし～したらあなたは気にしますか？」ですが、「～が～してもいいですか？」のニュアンスで、「許可」や「依頼」などを表しています。「大丈夫です」と言うつもりで Yes と答えると「はい、気にします」の意味になってしまいます。気にしない場合は No などで始まる答えが適切です。

🔊 48

3. Mark your answer on your answer sheet.　　Ⓐ Ⓑ Ⓒ

4. Mark your answer on your answer sheet.　　Ⓐ Ⓑ Ⓒ

5. Mark your answer on your answer sheet.　　Ⓐ Ⓑ Ⓒ

6. Mark your answer on your answer sheet.　　Ⓐ Ⓑ Ⓒ

Strategy for Part 3 ［会話問題の解き方］

2 人の会話問題 ④

　Part 3 では、音声の流れる順番に設問を解くヒントが出てくることが多いので、設問はほぼ上から順番に解くことができます。先読みが十分にできない場合でも、3 問セットの問題の 1 問目から解答するつもりで、音声を聞きながら集中して解きましょう。

Questions 7-9   🔊 49

7. What does the man's company encourage its employees to do?
   (A) Enroll in a seminar
   (B) Take some classes
   (C) Lounge in the lobby
   (D) Get flyers

8. Why does the woman say she can't take tennis classes?
   (A) She hates sports.
   (B) She has good stamina.
   (C) She doesn't have endurance.
   (D) Her hand is injured.

9. What does the man say he will do next?
   (A) Contact other employees
   (B) Send a wedding invitation
   (C) Organize a team-building event
   (D) Give his wife a gift

Part 4 Talks

スピーチ ②

　イベント準備に関するスピーチでは、学校、企業での行事、入会、入社、退職祝いなどが扱われます。イベントの内容、詳細説明やイベントに向けての注意事項について話が展開します。

Questions 10-12   ◀)) 50

10. Who most likely is the speaker?

(A) A professor

(B) An art student

(C) An events organizer

(D) A senior

11. Why should all items be properly labeled?

(A) To attract viewers

(B) To solicit support from benefactors

(C) To ensure safety

(D) To advertise their university

12. What should the listeners do for immediate concerns?

(A) Remove dangerous items

(B) Focus on the aesthetic of the exhibit

(C) Contact the project leader

(D) Call the district manager

Part 5 　Incomplete Sentences

Strategy for Part 5 ［短文穴埋め問題の解き方］

【文法問題 ③ 　代名詞】

　Part 5 の文法問題の中でも難易度が低く、選択肢には he / him / himself などの「（人称）代名詞」が並んでいるので、問題識別も容易です。では、色々な代名詞の用法を確認しましょう。

「人称代名詞のおさらい」

　代名詞には「格」の理解が必要です。「格」とは、名詞・代名詞と他の語句との関係を表す形のこと。つまり、文中での役割に応じた形を指します。名詞の場合、主格と目的格の形は同じです。

「主格」：主語になるときの形

　〔人称代名詞〕I / you / he / she / it / we / you / they

「所有格」：名詞を修飾し「〜の○○」という所有関係を示し、「所有格＋名詞」の形をとる

　◇人以外の単数名詞には「's」を付け、複数名詞には「s'」を付ける

　〔人称代名詞〕my / your / his / her / its / our / your / their

「目的格」：動詞や前置詞などの目的語の位置にくるときの形

　〔人称代名詞〕me / you / him / her / it / us / you / them

「所有代名詞」mine / yours / his / hers / ours / yours / theirs 　＊ただし、it を除く

　所有代名詞は「所有格＋名詞」が 1 つの単語になったもので、所有格と同じ働きをし、「〜のもの」の意味を表します。用法は、主に下記の 2 つです。

① 前後の（代）名詞を受ける場合

　例文 This racket is **hers**, but not **mine**. (hers = her racket, mine = my racket)
　　　（このラケットは彼女のもので、私のものではない。）

　これは同じ語（racket）の繰り返しを避けるためです。一般的によく使われる用法。

②「of ＋所有代名詞」の形でつかう場合

　例文 I have made it a habit to paint a used shirt **of mine** once a month.
　　　（月に一度、私の古着に絵を描くことを習慣にしている。）

　冠詞（a / the など）や限定詞（this / that / no / any / some / every など）と所有格を重ねて、「a my shirt」と言うことはできないので、「a shirt **of mine**」と表します。

「再帰代名詞」myself / yourself / himself / herself / itself / ourselves / yourselves /
　　　　　　　themselves

　再帰代名詞は、「〜自身」を意味します。1 人称と 2 人称は「所有格＋-self / -selves」、そして 3 人称は「目的格＋-self / -selves」で再帰代名詞の形になります。用法は、主に以下の 2 つです。

① 強調する場合

　例文 Luke has collected all these stamps **himself**.
　　　（ルーク自身がこれらすべての切手を集めた。）

　強調する語（主語、目的語、補語の名詞や代名詞）の直後に置いたり、例文のように文末に再帰代名詞を置き「〜自身が（で）」の意味を表し、「誰が」という意味を強めます。

② 動詞や前置詞の目的語になる場合

例文 She has decided to put **herself** into calligraphy for a school exhibition.

（彼女は、学校の展示会のために書道に打ち込むことに決めた。）

主語自身が、動詞や前置詞の目的語になる場合、主語の行為が主語自身に及ぶことを表す。

例題 The housewives attending in the gardening workshop learn how to raise herbs in ------- house.

(A) they   (B) their   (C) them   (D) theirs

解説 代名詞の問題は、空所前後から「（単数複数を含む）人称」と「格」を特定しましょう。今回の登場人物は the housewives（単数：housewife）なので、人称は「3 人称複数形」だとわかります。そして、空所直後の house という名詞を修飾する形が空所に入るので、「所有格」だと推測できます。したがって、「3 人称複数形の所有格」である **(B) their** が正解。

参考訳 園芸ワークショップに参加している主婦は、自宅でどのようにハーブを育てるかを学ぶ。

13. The amusement parks in America are much larger than ------- in countries in Asia.

(A) they   (B) that   (C) those   (D) there

14. Yesterday's couch shipment was too heavy for Mr. and Mrs. Pearson to move by -------.

(A) themselves   (B) them   (C) theirs   (D) their own

15. When harvesting fruits and vegetables, you had better not move sharp implements toward -------.

(A) yours   (B) your   (C) your own   (D) yourself

16. On behalf of local citizens, we express ------- deepest gratitude to the sponsors.

(A) us   (B) ours   (C) our   (D) we

17. When purchasing a laptop, customers are recommended to compare other models and prices before making up ------- own mind.

(A) their   (B) them   (C) themselves   (D) theirs

18. Despite the fact that Italian restaurants have expanded in town, customers still find ------- queueing for the best Italian food.

(A) it   (B) themselves   (C) itself   (D) they

19. Different from a motor-assisted revolving stage, actors and actresses in old ages had to rotate man-powered revolving stages by -------.

(A) their own   (B) theirs   (C) themselves   (D) them

20. Ms. Scavo, a staff at the box office, was able to count tickets faster as ------- learned tips from veteran staff.

(A) she   (B) her   (C) hers   (D) herself

21. We need to make sure that Ms. Huber has checked the rough design before we send ------- the completed patchwork quilt.

(A) herself   (B) her   (C) hers   (D) she

Part 6 Text Completion

Strategy for Part 6 ［長文穴埋め問題の解き方］

　Unit 6 で紹介した、「文脈に関係なく解ける問題」のうち「品詞問題」「前置詞を選ぶ問題」は頻出ではありませんが、出題されたときは、得点源だと思って、Part 5 の対策で身に付けた文法力を使って着実に正解に結び付けましょう。

Question 22-25 refer to the following announcement.

While inside the rehearsal room, all users are asked to ------ from eating, drinking, littering, or sleeping. Please ------ to leave the room clean and available for the next
22.　　　　　　　　　　　　　　　　23.
user. The usage of the piano in the practice rooms is timed and all those who wish to ------ should book one day in advance. ------. To book a time and date, please
24.　　　　　　　　　　　　　　　　　25.
visit our new website www.pianorooms.org.

22. (A) restrain　　　(B) refrain　　　(C) remain　　　(D) maintain

23. (A) keep　　　(B) make time　　　(C) ensure　　　(D) forget

24. (A) conserve　　　(B) see　　　(C) reserve　　　(D) contact

25. (A) Extension of time reservation can only be done online prior to arrival.
    (B) We will kick out those who cannot follow the rules of our music studio.
    (C) It is imperative for musicians to have discipline, especially with time.
    (D) We would like to accommodate all time extensions to help your mastery.

Strategy for Part 7 ［読解問題の解き方］

　Unit 3 で紹介した、Part 7 の設問のうち、「1．文書の目的・概要を問うタイプ」は、全体の流れをつかむ問題です。Part 7 を解く際には、ある程度の集中力を保って、文書をすべて読むことを目標にしましょう。

Questions 26 to 27 refer to the following e-mail.

From:	Jane Rutherford <j.rutherford@yakimonostudios.com>
To:	Yuki Takahashi <takahashi-yuki@webmail.com>
Date:	March 10
Subject:	Your Pottery Lessons

Dear Ms. Takahashi,

Thank you for your email regarding your interest to attend our pottery sessions this March. You may have seen our ads on the social media platforms and wanted to try out for the first batch. Unfortunately, the current batch slots have already been filled and we can no longer accommodate new enrollees.

However, we have a new batch this coming April starting April 1st. We have a renowned instructor coming in on that day as well, all the way from the U.S.A., who will be handling the sessions for the 2nd batch. Would you be interested in taking part in it?

Please let me know so I can immediately reserve your slot and proceed with the processing of your reservation. If you have any further questions, please don't hesitate to send me an email or call our studio at 1225-254-899.

Looking forward to your positive response!

Jane Rutherford
Yakimono Studios

26. What is the purpose of Ms. Rutherford's email?
    (A) To cancel a reservation
    (B) To send an invoice for payment
    (C) To respond to an inquiry
    (D) To promote their studio

27. In Paragraph 1 Line 1, the word "interest" has the closest meaning to:
    (A) advantage
    (B) curiosity
    (C) increased rate
    (D) none of the above

28. Why can't Yakimono Studios accommodate new enrollees for the first batch?
    (A) The shop is going bankrupt.
    (B) There are not enough enrollees.
    (C) There were too many registrants.
    (D) The instructor is unavailable.

29. What is implied about Yakimono Studios?
    (A) It is popular among hobbyists.
    (B) It has high pricing for lessons.
    (C) They only accept online reservations.
    (D) They only have American instructors.

30. What does Ms. Rutherford request from Ms. Takahashi?
    (A) To let her know soon if she would enroll
    (B) To pay her registration fee
    (C) To receive her call
    (D) To give her a positive feedback

UNIT **11**

Education

Vocabulary Check!

Choose an appropriate translation for the following words.

🔊)) 51

1. appreciate ( )	**2.** renovation ( )	**3.** foundation ( )
4. council ( )	**5.** thrive ( )	**6.** unwavering ( )
7. subject ( )	**8.** erratic ( )	**9.** influx ( )
10. eager ( )	**11.** supervise ( )	**12.** improve ( )
13. laboratory ( )	**14.** festival ( )	**15.** principal ( )

a. 揺るぎない	b. 熱心な	c. 改装	d. 改善する
e. 科目	f. 認める	g. 実験室	h. 不安定な
i. 校長	j. 繁栄する	k. 祭り	l. 創設
m. 委員会	n. 流入	o. 監督する	

🎧 Listening Section

Part 1 Photographs

Strategy for Part 1 [写真描写問題の解き方]

教育の写真

　教育の写真では、教室内や会議室でのやりとり、運動場、学校行事を写真で表現していることが多く、先生や生徒たち、教室、学校、図書館、大学のキャンパス、校庭の遊具などが写真に写っているものが頻出されます。

1. 🔊 52

2.

Part 2 Question-Response

Strategy for Part 2 ［応答問題の解き方］

否定疑問文など ① Don't ~ ?, Isn't ~ ?などで始まる否定疑問文

Don't you ~ ?, Aren't you ~ ?, Isn't he ~ ?などには「~でないの？」「私はこう思うんだけど、あなたは違うの？」というニュアンスが含まれます。多少の不満などの気持ちがあるとイメージしましょう。

🔊 53

3. Mark your answer on your answer sheet. Ⓐ Ⓑ Ⓒ

4. Mark your answer on your answer sheet. Ⓐ Ⓑ Ⓒ

5. Mark your answer on your answer sheet. Ⓐ Ⓑ Ⓒ

6. Mark your answer on your answer sheet. Ⓐ Ⓑ Ⓒ

Strategy for Part 3 ［会話問題の解き方］

2人の会話問題 ⑤

　Part 3 の設問には「～というときに男性／女性は何を意味していますか」という意味を推測する問題が含まれています。この場合も会話の流れから、どのような意味でその発言をしたのか考えて答えましょう。

Questions 7-9   🔊 54

7. What event is taking place?
   (A) A feeding program
   (B) A ground-breaking ceremony
   (C) A visiting event
   (D) A house-warming party

8. According to the man, what was being constructed?
   (A) A trophy showcase hall
   (B) A new meeting hall
   (C) A bird wing
   (D) A club room

9. What does the woman mean when she says, "you have your work cut out for you"?
   (A) The construction time is lessened.
   (B) The renovation is a difficult task.
   (C) The principal needs to cut his work period.
   (D) The students are happy to have new club rooms.

Part 4 Talks

Strategy for Part 4 ［説明文問題の解き方］

スピーチ ③

　社内、組織内でのスピーチでは、プレゼンテーション、会議、授賞式の司会者のスピーチなども出題されます。その他にも組織内での功績に関して、メンバーを労う場面のパターンもあります。

Questions 10-12　　　　　　　　　　　　　　　　　　　🔊 55

10. What does the speaker thank the listeners for?
    (A) Their contribution to the success of the event
    (B) Their attendance to the event
    (C) Their visit to the school
    (D) Their promotion of the festival

11. What does the speaker say about the preparations for the event?
    (A) It was very tiring.
    (B) It made her conscious.
    (C) It was worth the money.
    (D) It was not fun.

12. What will the listeners probably do next year?
    (A) Mark their calendars
    (B) Label some places
    (C) Set up new stalls
    (D) Supervise all the students

Part 5 Incomplete Sentences

Strategy for Part 5 ［短文穴埋め問題の解き方］

【文法問題 ④ 関係代名詞】

　関係代名詞は「代名詞」と「接続詞」の両方の働きをします。つまり、代名詞のように「格」を
もち、関係代名詞に置き換えられた**名詞（先行詞）**を基準に、2 つの文を 1 つにする機能があります。
「（代）名詞」のように、文において**主語**や**目的語**になれます。常に、どちらの役割かを意識して学習
しましょう。

「関係代名詞が主格のとき：who / which / that」

例文 Dr. Phil **who** had been working for two decades was finally appointed as a chairman.

　　（20 年間働いているフィル博士は、ようやく主任教授（学科長）に任命された。）

　この文は ① Dr. Phil was finally appointed as a chairman. ② Dr. Phil had been working for two
decades. に分けることができ、共通する名詞（先行詞）は、Dr. Phil です。②でその名詞は「主語」
なので、「**主格の who**」に置き換えます。そして、①の先行詞の直後に移動することで形容詞的に先
行詞を説明することができます。

【見分け方】主格の関係代名詞の後ろには、必ず動詞がきます。

「関係代名詞が目的格のとき：who(m) / which / that」

例文 Acrylic boards have to be attached to all the desks **which** the school purchased.

　　（その学校が購入したすべての机に、アクリル板を取り付けなければならない。）

　この文は ① Acrylic boards have to be attached to all the desks. ② The school purchased the
desks. の 2 文から成っています。共通する名詞（先行詞）は、the desks です。②の文でその名詞は
動詞 purchase の目的語になっているので、「**目的格の which**」に置き換えます。そして、①の先行
詞の直後に置き、2 文を 1 文にします。

**【見分け方】目的格の関係代名詞の後ろには、主語と名詞があり、目的語位置に名詞がありません（"穴"
になっています）。**

「関係代名詞が所有格のとき：whose / whose」

例文 University recruited an applicant **whose** teaching skills stood out among all the
candidates.

　　（大学は、その指導能力が全候補者の中で目立っていた応募者を採用した。）

　この文は ① University recruited an applicant. ② His / Her teaching skills stood out among all
candidates. の 2 文から成っています。所有格の場合、「誰の（何の）名詞」なのかを考える必要が
あります。名詞 teaching skill は an applicant が所有するものと考えられるので、②にあるように「所
有格の His / Her」が付加されます。この場合、His / Her を「所有格 whose」に置換し、①の先行詞
の直後に移動することで 2 文を 1 文にすることができます。

**【見分け方】所有格の関係代名詞の後ろには、「所有格とセットになる名詞」があります。（「所有格＋
名詞」は主語にも目的語にもなれる、ということに注意しましょう）**

「関係代名詞 that が好まれるとき」

that を使う必要があるときは、主に以下の３つです。選択肢に that があるときは注意しましょう。

① 先行詞が「人と物」の場合

② 先行詞に最上級や「first / only / very」などが付いている場合

③ 先行詞が「all / anything / nothing / little / much / nothing」の場合

例文 The college is **the only** school **that** has introduced a distance learning on social welfare.
（その大学は、社会福祉の通信教育を導入している唯一の学校である。）

例題 Symposium attendees ------- confirm their attendance early will have a chance to talk to the keynote speaker before it starts.

(A) who　　　　(B) whose　　　　(C) whom　　　　(D) which

解説 まず、空所の後ろを確認しましょう。動詞 confirm とその目的語 their attendance があることから、この空所には主語の役割を担う、主格の関係代名詞が入ると推測できます。また、先行詞になる名詞は、attendees「参加者」なので、人以外の場合に使う (D) which ではなく、**(A) who** が正解。また、(B) whose は空所の後ろに所有関係が成立する名詞がない、(C) whom は動詞の後ろに目的語がすでにあるので目的格は使えない、という点でそれぞれ不正解になります。

参考訳 出席を早くに確認したシンポジウム参加者には、開始前に基調演説者と話す機会がある。

---

13. When recruiting staff for the open positions, universities should choose the ones ------- CVs are clearly and concisely written.

(A) who　　　　(B) whose　　　　(C) whom　　　　(D) which

14. The head teacher emphasizes the necessity of interpersonal communication for school personnel ------- jobs involve interaction with students and parents.

(A) whom　　　　(B) that　　　　(C) who　　　　(D) whose

15. Employees ------- have worked in the Administrative Office for more than 5 years will be subject to transferring to another department.

(A) whom　　　　(B) which　　　　(C) who　　　　(D) whose

16. All the language lecturers ------- have a class on the 1st period are allowed to leave the campus earlier than 5 o'clock.

(A) that　　　　(B) who　　　　(C) whom　　　　(D) whose

17. The university has decided that those ------- are with an identification card are eligible to enter the campus.

(A) whose　　　　(B) who　　　　(C) which　　　　(D) what

18. A liberal arts education extends beyond academia and the job to offer students the necessary qualities ------- allow them to thrive in this world.

(A) it   (B) whose   (C) who   (D) that

19. One fifth of the students will register remedial education ------- primary purpose is to assist students to achieve expected competencies in academic English.

(A) their   (B) whom   (C) whose   (D) which

20. Despite the absence from the lecture last week, Mikc found that there was nothing ------- he needed to catch up with.

(A) whom   (B) that   (C) who   (D) whose

21. Due to the influx of students, the university has received lots of complaints that there are few booths ------- are available for speaking practice all day.

(A) who   (B) which   (C) whose   (D) that

Part 6 **Text Completion**

Strategy for Part 6 ［長文穴埋め問題の解き方］

Part 6 で出題される「前置詞を選ぶ問題」のためには、「前置詞 + 名詞」「動詞 + 前置詞」「形容詞 + 前置詞」などのようにフレーズで覚える習慣を身に付けておくと得点アップに役立ちます。

Question 22-25 refer to the following e-mail.

To: Mrs. Kelly Chambre <kellychambre@mailweb.com>
From: Ms. Nadia Marquez <n.marquez@wellingtonschool.edu.com>
Date: August 23
Subject: Parents-Teachers' Association Election

Dear Mrs. Chambre,

We'd like to thank you for your ------ support to our PTA time and time again. You
22.
have always supported our school in making our system conducive for learning
and growing. Your children are also very helpful in the student council and we
couldn't be any happier to have their help as well as yours.

------, we will be having a PTA Election for the upcoming school year on August
23.
30th. ------. Other parents also recognize your contributions to the school, so we
24.
decided to ask you formally regarding the matter.

We ------ hearing from you.
25.
As always, thank you for your contributions to making our school a better place for
the children.

Sincerely,

Nadia Marquez
Principal, Wellington School

22. (A) unwavering   (B) erratic   (C) inconsistent   (D) unreliable

23. (A) Now   (B) Then   (C) Usually   (D) Relatively

24. (A) We would like to ask if you would be interested in running for president in the
     election this time.
    (B) We would like to know if you're still interested in helping our school.
    (C) We want to know if you can make it to the school's foundation day.
    (D) We are hoping if you can be of help in the activity for our grade-schoolers.

25. (A) look at
    (B) look back on
    (C) look forward to
    (D) look towards

Unit 3 で紹介した Part 7 の設問の種類のうち、「6. 単語の意味を問うタイプ」は Part 7 の全 54 問中、5 問程度出題されます。解答にあまり時間はかかりませんが、単語の意味だけを考えるのではなく、文脈にあてはめてから解答してみましょう。

Questions 26 to 30 refer to the following suggestion form.

Bentley University

Student Name: Hannah Ferguson

Date: June 12

Contact Number: 154-887-9988

Comment:

Last week, we had our mock examinations for the upcoming Midterms. I was able to get a better score this time compared to my Preliminary tests, and I was surprised at how the improvement came unexpected. I would like to extend my gratitude to Mr. Kamado who patiently taught our class and who made sure everyone was able to understand the lesson materials in our Calculus subject. Everyone would agree that we all believed we would flunk the mock right after the initial examinations, but our professors were able to motivate us to study and believe that we will be able to make it through to the following tests. If I may suggest, I hope our school can allow group tutorials and reviews with our professors, if possible, since there are many major subjects that require more guidance outside our regular classes.

---

26. What is most likely true based on the information in the meeting?

(A) Most professors are incompetent.

(B) Bentley University's dance hall is of high quality.

(C) Examinations are impossible to pass.

(D) Professors in Bentley University are dedicated to teaching their students well.

27. What type of subject does Mr. Kamado teach?

(A) English

(B) Mathematics

(C) Science

(D) Art

28. The word "flunk" in line 6 is closest in meaning to

(A) pass

(B) fail

(C) perfect

(D) forget

29. What is implied about Hannah Ferguson?

(A) She is a hard-working student.

(B) She only cares about passing her tests.

(C) She prefers to have one-on-one sessions with her professors.

(D) She doesn't care about her grades.

30. Why does Hannah Ferguson suggest group tutorials with their professors?

(A) Because everyone will fail if they don't have group tutorials

(B) So that their professors can guide them further in their studies

(C) So that all the students can have fun with their teachers

(D) Because she thinks the professors aren't teaching well enough

Sports

Vocabulary Check!

Choose an appropriate translation for the following words.

🔊 56

1. membership (　)	**2.** congratulate (　)	**3.** decisive (　)
4. anxiety (　)	**5.** constant (　)	**6.** publish (　)
7. hospitalize (　)	**8.** absolutely (　)	**9.** gym (　)
10. injury (　)	**11.** solidify (　)	**12.** outskirts (　)
13. questionnaire (　)	**14.** explore (　)	**15.** advertisement (　)

a. 絶対に	b. 決定的な	c. 団結させる	d. 探索する
e. 継続した	f. 祝う	g. 広告	h. 入院させる
i. 郊外	j. アンケート	k. 負傷	l. 会員
m. 心配	n. ジム	o. 出版する	

🎧 Listening Section

Part 1　Photographs

Strategy for Part 1 ［写真描写問題の解き方］

スポーツの写真

　スポーツの写真では、「彼らは野球をしている」「彼らはサッカーをしている」のようにスポーツ名は何か？について識別するのではなく、実際に「ボールを持っている」、「バットを振っている」、「球を追いかけている」のような、一つ一つの動作が示されていることが多いです。

1. 🔊 57

Ⓐ Ⓑ Ⓒ Ⓓ

2.

Ⓐ Ⓑ Ⓒ Ⓓ

Part 2 Question-Response

Strategy for Part 2 ［応答問題の解き方］

否定疑問文など ②　付加疑問文

　設問の最後が ~ don't you?, ~ is it?, ~ isn't it? などで終わり、「ですよね？」「ではないですよね？」と確認するのが付加疑問文です。否定疑問文、付加疑問文の考え方は同じで、例えばDidn't you say ~ ?「言わなかったの？」に対して、「言った」なら Yes (I did).「言わなかった」なら No (I didn't). で答えます。

🔊 58

3. Mark your answer on your answer sheet.　Ⓐ Ⓑ Ⓒ

4. Mark your answer on your answer sheet.　Ⓐ Ⓑ Ⓒ

5. Mark your answer on your answer sheet.　Ⓐ Ⓑ Ⓒ

6. Mark your answer on your answer sheet.　Ⓐ Ⓑ Ⓒ

3人の会話 ②

　登場人物の男性または女性のどちらかが2人となる場合、先に設問を読んでおくことでどちらが複数なのか見分けることが可能です。設問に men とあれば、男性が複数、women とあれば女性が複数になるとわかります。また、設問の主語に男性の名前、女性の名前が出てきている場合、その性別が複数である可能性が高いです。

Questions 7-9　　　🔊 59

7.　According to the woman, what happened to one of their members?

(A) She went out.

(B) She passed the exam.

(C) She quit the team.

(D) She fainted.

8.　What does the man say might happen?

(A) The team would win the competition.

(B) The team's performance might be affected.

(C) The competition would be canceled.

(D) The coach will be hospitalized.

9.　What does Marco mean when he says, "It's probably the anxiety that pushed her to practice beyond her limits"?

(A) The team member was unhealthy.

(B) The competition was pressuring.

(C) The worry pushed the team member to quit.

(D) The team member was not capable.

Part 4 Talks

Strategy for Part 4 ［説明文問題の解き方］

音声メッセージ ③

　音声メッセージでは、冒頭で話し手の情報が得られます。続く文で本題に入り、起こった出来事、伝えたい情報、そしてメッセージを終える前に、（「次回会いましょう」、「連絡をください」など）聞き手に何らかの希望が伝えられます。

Questions 10-12　　　　🔊 60

10. Why is the speaker most likely calling?
    (A) To congratulate a member's recovery
    (B) To apologize for an accident
    (C) To ask a member to return
    (D) To charge a member a fee

11. What does the speaker say about the accident?
    (A) It is rare.
    (B) It usually happens among players.
    (C) It is uncommon.
    (D) It happens among spectators.

12. What does the speaker advise the listener to do?
    (A) To take things easy
    (B) To work harder
    (C) To rehabilitate the team
    (D) To overcome fears

Part 5　Incomplete Sentences

Strategy for Part 5 ［短文穴埋め問題の解き方］

【文法問題 ⑤　関係副詞】

「関係副詞」は、関係代名詞と間違うケースが多いので、前の UNIT と合わせて、確認していきましょう。

「関係代名詞のおさらい」

関係代名詞は、「接続詞」と「（代）名詞」の両方の働きをします。つまり、2 つの文を 1 つの文に結ぶことができるのです。また、代名詞のように「格」によって形が変化します。（代）名詞が関係代名詞に置き換わるので、関係代名詞の後ろには**不完全な文**が続きます。

先行詞	主格	所有格	目的格
人	who	whose	who(m)
物	which	whose	which
人・物	that	―	that

「関係副詞」

関係副詞も「接続詞」と同じ働きをするので、2 つの文を 1 つの文につなぐことができます。ただし、名詞ではなく「**副詞／＊前置詞＋名詞**」を置き換える役割があります。副詞（句）は文型の一部にならない付加的な要素ということから、関係副詞の後ろには常に**完全文**が続きます。

例文 ① The tournament is held in the stadium.
　　　（その大会は、そのスタジアムで開催される。）

例文 ② Ninety thousand people are accommodated **there**.
　　　（そこでは 9 万人が収容できる。）

　この 2 文で共通している単語を考えてみましょう。「**there**」は「**in the stadium**」と表すことができるので、「the stadium」が先行詞になります。there を「**関係副詞 where**」に置換し、先行詞「the stadium」の後ろに移動させ、2 つの文を接続します。この時、where 以下は SV を含む完全文になっています。

①＋② The tournament is held in the stadium **where** ninety thousand people are accommodated.
　　　（その大会は、9 万人が収容できるスタジアムで開催される。）

「関係副詞の種類」

① **where**（場所）先行詞の例：the place, the situation, the area（＝副詞 there で表せる場所や空間）

② **when**（時）　　先行詞の例：the time, the day（＝副詞 then で表せる時や時間）

③ **why**（理由）　先行詞の例：the reason

④ **how**（方法）　先行詞の例：the way（"the way how" とは言わないことに注意）

例題 Computers have changed ------- businesses work, people play, and the world communicates.

(A) what   (B) which   (C) in which   (D) how

解説 空所の前には、先行詞となる名詞がありません。つまり、(B) which や (C) in which のように関係代名詞を含む選択肢は、どの名詞を先行詞としているかがわからないため不正解となります。また、(A) what は他動詞の目的語になるはずですが、空所の後ろの動詞はすべて自動詞であることから、what を目的語として取ることができません。よって、先行詞（the way）とは一緒に用いない関係副詞である **(D) how** が正解。

参考訳 コンピュータは、ビジネスの仕組みや人々の遊び方、世界のコミュニケーションの取り方を変えてきた。

---

13. The athletic park ------- the sports event for children is going to be held is on the outskirts of Nagoya.

(A) whose   (B) in that   (C) where   (D) when

14. The monthly sport magazine is requesting that Olympic medalists complete a survey detailing ------- their daily training consists of.

(A) what   (B) how   (C) whose   (D) when

15. The city hall, ------- has undergone extensive renovations, will reopen this month.

(A) where   (B) when   (C) who   (D) which

16. Top shoe companies always know ------- their rivals are doing in order to stay competitive.

(A) what   (B) that   (C) how   (D) whether

17. A popular destination in Malaysia is beautiful Cameron National Park, ------- travelers can explore historic tea plantations and enjoy the fresh mountain air.

(A) that   (B) which   (C) what   (D) where

18. The bistro ------- we had lunch with the clients last week has been closed by health inspectors.

(A) which   (B) where   (C) whose   (D) when

19. The registration fee for the fitness membership will be charged at the end of this month, ------- rental fees of training shoes will also be billed together.

(A) which   (B) whose   (C) when   (D) where

20. Susan Cook, ------- latest book was published in July, has given up her career as an office manager to become a full-time novelist.

(A) whose   (B) in which   (C) when   (D) where

21. The racket maker, ------- is now located downtown, is considering relocation of its offices to the outskirts of Fukuoka because most of its workers and clients live there.

(A) when   (B) who   (C) which   (D) in which

Part 6   Text Completion

Strategy for Part 6 ［長文穴埋め問題の解き方］

TOEIC 受験者の大半にとって、Reading Section は特に時間との闘いです。Part 7 の問題は全 54 問という最も大きなパートですから、Part 5 と Part 6 にかける時間は極力短くする必要があります。そのためには「メール」「お知らせ」「手紙」「社内観覧」はどのように書かれているのか試験前に少しでもチェックしておくことが有効です。

Question 22-25 refer to the following e-mail.

To: Danny Alvarez <dannysoccer@webpost.com>
From: Dr. Park Soo-ah <park-soo-ah@princehospital.com>
Date: January 12
Subject: Your Annual Checkup

Dear Mr. Alvarez,

Your last game with the Roaring Thunders was a ------- win, and I would like to
    22.
congratulate you on becoming the champion of this year's National Cup. Your team has solidified its teamwork after 3 years of constant practice.

Now that the big game has been -------, I would like to let you know that our office is
    23.
open for your annual medical checkup anytime next month. -------. Still, I hope you
    24.
will be able to see me as soon as possible since you mentioned you had an -------
    25.
pain in the left thigh during your last match.

Please let me know when you'd like to have your tests and checkup scheduled.

I am looking forward to seeing you in February.

Kind regards,

Dr. Park Soo-ah
Prince Hospital

22. (A) initial   (B) unsure   (C) decisive   (D) unreliable

23. (A) concluded   (B) started   (C) decided   (D) announced

24. (A) You can come into my office any time you want.
    (B) This will be your last checkup with me as your attending physician.
    (C) We understand that you will need some time to attend social events and homecoming parties upon arriving here.
    (D) Please set an appointment online.

25. (A) unbeatable   (B) unbearable   (C) unbelievable   (D) unlucky

Questions 26 to 30 refer to the following advertisement and e-mail.

Pre-opening Discounts at Arlington Gym

Good news!

We're planning further expansion of our gyms in the Arizona area starting July this year, and as a special treat to all those interested in our early bird sign-up, we have a pleasant surprise for the first 50 applicants who want to start their fitness journey with us!

Our regular membership rate starts at $35 per month, but if you sign up before June 30th, we will give you a 10% discount, plus freebies such as gym bag, a yoga mat, and many more!

Ready to start becoming more fit and healthy?
Go to our website at www.arlington-gym@.com and fill out the form for the new Arizona branch! See you there!

To:	<arlington-gym@webcord.com>
From:	Kent McKenzie <kent.mckzie@nettle.com>
Date:	July 2
Subject:	Inquiry on Early Bird Signup

Good day.
I saw your advertisement about the early bird promo just earlier and hope I'm not too late to avail. I've been a member of your gym in Texas but had to stop due to my relocation to Canada, and now I have returned to my home state Arizona. I saw your ad posted on your website. Are there any slots left? I really hope I make it since I also heard from my fitness coach that he will be transferring to the Phoenix branch once the construction is finished.

Looking forward to a positive response.
Thank you!

Sincerely,
Kent McKenzie

26. What is indicated about the gym membership in the advertisement?
(A) It is expensive.
(B) It will be discounted for late enrollees.
(C) There are perks for those who will sign up early.
(D) There are free items included in their regular membership.

27. How will inquirers sign up?
(A) By going to their Arizona office
(B) By sending a letter to the gym
(C) By accomplishing an online questionnaire
(D) By calling their telephone number

28. What is implied about Kent McKenzie?
(A) He was a regular in Arlington Gym.
(B) He quit going to the gym due to an injury.
(C) He decided to move to another country to cancel his gym membership.
(D) He is not satisfied with the gym's facilities.

29. Why does Mr. McKenzie send an email?
(A) He wants to know if his coach will be transferred to the Phoenix branch.
(B) He wants a refund of his previous gym membership fee.
(C) He wants to know of the availability of the promo he saw on the gym's website.
(D) He wants to know if he's eligible to become a member of the gym.

30. How will the gym most likely respond to his email?
(A) His request may be turned down because of the deadline.
(B) He will be able to avail of the promo.
(C) His request will be accepted since he is very early to sign up.
(D) He will be accepted since he knows a gym coach from a different branch.

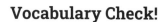

UNIT 13

Hospital

Vocabulary Check!

Choose an appropriate translation for the following words.

🔊 61

1. mandatory ( )	**2.** veterinarian ( )	**3.** pharmacist ( )
4. consultation ( )	**5.** medicine ( )	**6.** cardiovascular ( )
7. ingredient ( )	**8.** ensure ( )	**9.** portable ( )
10. relocation ( )	**11.** limitation ( )	**12.** stethoscope ( )
13. stationery ( )	**14.** clinic ( )	**15.** adjustment ( )

a. 聴診器	b. 移転	c. 強制的な	d. 獣医
e. 文具	f. 持ち運びできる	g. 材料	h. 制限
i. 心臓血管の	j. 調整	k. 診察	l. 医院
m. 薬剤師	n. 確実にする	o. 薬	

🎧 Listening Section

Part 1 Photographs

Strategy for Part 1 ［写真描写問題の解き方］

医療の写真

　病院、医療の写真では、hospital, doctor, patient などの単語の他に、medicine, mask, operation, prescription, treatment なども頻出します。

1. 🔊 62

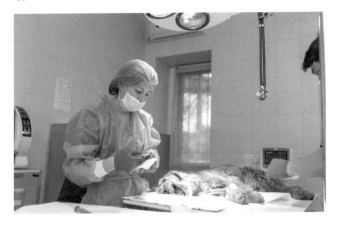

Ⓐ Ⓑ Ⓒ Ⓓ

2.

Ⓐ Ⓑ Ⓒ Ⓓ

Part 2 **Question-Response**

Strategy for Part 2 ［応答問題の解き方］

否定疑問文など ③　AかBか選ぶ選択疑問文

　設問中にA or Bという、「AかBか」の表現が入る選択疑問文は必然的に設問文が長くなり、難しく感じるかもしれませんが、答えのパターンを学習しておきましょう。正解のパターンとして「Aのみ」「Bのみ」「どちらでもよい」「どちらも不可」「まだ決まっていない」などがあります。

🔊 63

3. Mark your answer on your answer sheet. Ⓐ Ⓑ Ⓒ

4. Mark your answer on your answer sheet. Ⓐ Ⓑ Ⓒ

5. Mark your answer on your answer sheet. Ⓐ Ⓑ Ⓒ

6. Mark your answer on your answer sheet. Ⓐ Ⓑ Ⓒ

Part 3 **Conversations**

> **Strategy for Part 3** ［会話問題の解き方］
>
> **図表を含む問題 ③**
>
> 　図表を含む問題では、必ず音声と図表の内容の両方から正解を導き出すようになっています。まず は図表に示されている数字や文字をすばやくチェックして、その数や名詞などが聞こえてくるのを待 ち構えながら聞きましょう。

Questions 7-9　　　　　　　　　　　　　　　　　　　　　　　　　 64

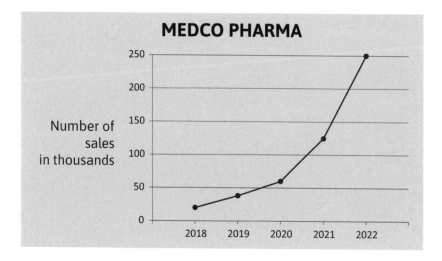

7. What does the man mean when he says, "I think we fare quite well"?
   (A) Their company can keep up with their competitors.
   (B) The industry is unstable.
   (C) Business is not doing well.
   (D) He thinks the world is unfair.

8. Look at the graphic. In what year did the woman say they made the most sales?
   (A) 2019
   (B) 2020
   (C) 2021
   (D) 2022

9. What problem does the man mention?
   (A) Creating a new type of medicine
   (B) Selling their new drug
   (C) Developing a marketing team
   (D) Helping all patients

Part 4 Talks

Questions 10-12   🔊 65

10. When will the clinic be closed?

(A) On the 16th

(B) On the 17th

(C) On the 18th

(D) On the 19th

11. According to the speaker, when should the listeners set their mandatory appointments?

(A) On the day of the conference

(B) Right before or after the conference

(C) Three days after the conference

(D) A week after the conference

12. What does the speaker suggest the listeners do?

(A) Call the receptionist for urgent concerns

(B) Forward their number to the doctors

(C) Call the doctors

(D) Ignore their concern

Part 5 Incomplete Sentences

Strategy for Part 5 ［短文穴埋め問題の解き方］

【文法問題 ⑥ 比較・最上級】

「比較級・最上級」の問題では、「～と同じくらい…だ」「～より…だ」「～で一番…だ」といった基本形だけではなく、様々な表現が出題されます。特徴として、選択肢には more や most などの比較級・最上級を表す語句が並んでいるので、空所位置と than などの目印となる語句を必ず確認しましょう。

* Part 5 では、than を選ぶ問題も時折出題されています。

「比較級のおさらい」

2 つのものを比べて「A は B より、もっと～／より～である（～する）」という意味を表し、基本的に以下の形を用います。形容詞・副詞が 2 音節以上のものには、-er ではなく、more / less を付けます。

形容詞の基本形：**A is (形容詞＋ -er) than B (is). / A is more (less) 形容詞 than B (is).**
副詞の基本形：**A do (副詞＋ -er) than B (do). / A do more (less) 副詞 than B (do).**

比較級の問題でよく出題されるパターン

The ＋比較級＋ SV ～ , the ＋比較級＋ SV ～ . 「～すればするほど、ますます…である（する）」

例文 The higher you climb, the colder the air becomes.
（高く登れば登るほど、ますます空気は冷たくなる。）

比較級を修飾する語句　 * Part 5 では、比較級の意味を強める語句を選ぶ問題も出題されています。

例文にあるように、修飾語は比較級の前に置きます。強調の度合いが異なるので注意が必要です。

例文 My father speaks **much** faster than my mother does.
（私の父は母よりもとても早く喋ります。）

a bit / a little bit	rather / somewhat	far / much / a lot	even / still / yet
「少し」	「やや」	「とても」	「いっそう」

「最上級のおさらい」

3 つ以上のものを比べて「A は…の中で最も～だ（～する）」という意味を表します。the family / the country など**範囲や場所**を表す場合は in を使い、the boys / the three など**複数名詞や数**を表す場合は of が使われます。また、形容詞・副詞が 2 音節以上の場合は、-est ではなく、most / least を付けます。

形容詞の基本形：**A is the (形容詞＋ -est) in (of) ～ . / A is the most (least) 形容詞 in (of) ～ .**
副詞の基本形：**A do the (副詞＋ -est) in (of) ～ . / A do the most (least) 副詞 in (of) ～ .**

最上級を修飾する語句

最上級と比較級では強調のために使われる語句が異なります。**最上級で使われるのは主に by far / much / yet（ずば抜けて、はるかに）**です。しっかりと区別して学習しましょう。

例文 Mr. Jones speaks **by far** the fastest of all the teachers.
（ジョーンズ先生はすべての教員の中で、ずば抜けて一番早く喋ります。）

例題 Many hospitals use fluorescent bulbs because they are six time ------- than incandescent bulbs.

(A) as efficient　　　(B) most efficiently　(C) so efficiently　　(D) more efficient

解説　空所に形容詞、副詞のどちらが入るかを識別しましょう。Because 節の主語 they と動詞 are から判断すると、空所には補語となる形容詞が入ると考えられます。したがって、副詞である (B) と (C) は不正解。また、文中には原級（同じくらい…だ）を表す as がないため、(A) as efficient も不正解 となります。よって、文中の than とともに用いることのできる (D) more efficient が正解。

参考訳　蛍光灯は白熱灯よりも６倍効率が良いので、多くの病院が使用している。

13. The recently released oral drag is spreading ------- faster than had been predicted.
(A) more　　　　(B) too　　　　(C) very　　　　(D) much

14. Using a portable heater to heat a smaller room at night is probably the ------- way to save big on your power bill.
(A) most easiest　(B) easy　　　(C) more easily　(D) easiest

15. Nurses on the night shift are likely to make three times ------- mistakes as their colleagues on the day shift.
(A) as more　　　(B) as many　　(C) as much　　(D) more

16. The copy machines at the dispensing pharmacy malfunction ------- than computers do.
(A) more frequently　(B) more frequent　(C) most frequent　(D) most frequently

17. Mr. Lege states that his products have such a high quality because the ------- judgement of them is his own.
(A) harsher　　　(B) harshest　　(C) harshly　　(D) more harshly

18. The combination of experienced workers and the cutting-edge automatic checkout machines ensures that the Central Hospital is ------- to its rivals.
(A) better　　　(B) superior　　(C) advanced　　(D) improved

19. The Metropolitan Clinic has the ------- respected cardiovascular surgeon in the city.
(A) high　　　　(B) better　　　(C) most　　　　(D) favorable

20. A study conducted recently showed that, statistically, day laborers did not make nearly ------- errors as night workers.

(A) as many (B) much more (C) more than (D) too much

21. Many products now use plastics in place of wood as they can be ------- more impact-resistant.

(A) very (B) many (C) much (D) as

Part 6 Text Completion

Strategy for Part 6 ［長文穴埋め問題の解き方］

Part 6 の設問「文脈に沿って解く問題」のうち、「動詞の形を選ぶ問題」では、「過去形」「現在形」「未来表現」「現在完了形」のどれが選択肢に並んでいるのか、まず確認して、文全体の時制と合わせて考えましょう。

Question 22-25 refer to the following announcement.

To all our pharmacists and staff:

Please be advised that our current shipment schedule ------- starting next month.
22.
The adjustment is because of shipping delays all across the country, and this affects all our branches nationwide. All those in charge of inventory should take note that deliveries will be done ------- Tuesday, 5 o'clock in the afternoon.
23.
To our pharmacists, keep the schedule in mind to inform our regular customers in case their medicine goes -------.
24.
-------. Thank you.
25.

---

22. (A) change
(B) is changing
(C) has been changed
(D) will be changed

23. (A) in (B) on (C) every (D) for

24. (A) out of stock   (B) modified   (C) off the rack   (D) well

25. (A) For your understanding.
     (B) For your compliance.
     (C) For your feedback.
     (D) For your signature.

Part 7 Single Passages / Multiple Passages

Strategy for Part 7 ［読解問題の解き方］

　Part 7 の「ダブル・パッセージ型」の設問のうち、両方の文書からヒントを見つけないと解けない問題は1、2問だと Unit 6 で解説しました。その他のどちらか一方の文書で解ける問題は「According to the e-mail」など、どちらの文書にヒントがあるのかを示す語句で始まっていることも多いです。効率よくヒントを見つけましょう。

Questions 26 to 30 refer to the following notice and e-mail.

Notice

April 10

To all our patients:

In order to serve you better, our clinic will be undergoing a renovation and a series of disinfection in the next two months. Your health is our main concern, and because of this, we will be closing the clinic for in-person checkups. In lieu of the face-to-face consultations, we will be booking appointments through e-checkups. This can be done through calling 009-187-8876, or you can log in at our online booking system at www.medservices-altomed.com.

If you need any assistance in navigating through the website, feel free to send us an email at altomed@medserv.com and our staff will be happy to help you.

We apologize for any inconvenience this may cause.
We look forward to seeing you again in July.

Richard Cummings
Receptionist, Alto Med Clinic

Date:	April 11
To:	altomed@medserv.com
From:	Brittany Skye <britskye@messan.com>

Dear Mr. Cummings,

Thank you for giving us information about the changes in the clinic. My grandmother is scheduled to have her next checkup in May, and this will fall under the renovation period. I tried to check your website and it is very user-friendly so I didn't have any trouble setting up a schedule. However, I had some difficulty in the payment system, and I couldn't seem to input my payment details. I hope one of your team members can assist me with this.

Thank you and hope to hear from you soon.

Best,
Brittany Skye

26. What will be done in the next two months?
   (A) A recompensation
   (B) A reconstruction
   (C) A relocation
   (D) A recognition

27. In paragraph 1, line 3 of the notice, what does "in lieu of" mean?
   (A) in front of
   (B) in place of
   (C) in line with
   (D) in consideration of

28. What can be inferred about Ms. Skye?
   (A) She is a patient in the clinic.
   (B) She likes Mr. Cummings.
   (C) She takes care of her grandmother.
   (D) She doesn't have enough money.

29. What issue did Ms. Skye encounter?

   (A) A problem in registering a payment

   (B) A concern in the scheduling system

   (C) A bug in her computer

   (D) A double-charged payment

30. Who will assist Ms. Skye?

   (A) A staff person

   (B) A doctor

   (C) A receptionist

   (D) A construction worker

UNIT 14

Employment

Vocabulary Check!

Choose an appropriate translation for the following words.　🔊 66

1. currently (　　)　　2. simultaneously (　　)　　3. suitable (　　)

4. due (　　)　　5. innovative (　　)　　6. checklist (　　)

7. submit (　　)　　8. recruit (　　)　　9. applicant (　　)

10. load (　　)　　11. treatment (　　)　　12. receptionist (　　)

13. compliance (　　)　　14. awareness (　　)　　15. plausible (　　)

a. 同時に	b. 積む	c. 採用する	d. 気づき
e. 妥当な	f. 締め切りの	g. 受付係	h. 革新的な
i. 治療する	j. 確認リスト	k. 遵守すること	l. 現在は
m. 適している	n. 提出する	o. 志願者	

🎧 Listening Section

Part 1　Photographs

Strategy for Part 1［写真描写問題の解き方］

雇用の写真

　雇用の写真では、職場や役職が明らかな場面や、就職活動、面接、学生がスーツを着ている場面などが出題されます。

1. 🔊 67

Ⓐ Ⓑ Ⓒ Ⓓ

2.

Ⓐ Ⓑ Ⓒ Ⓓ

Part 2 Question-Response

Strategy for Part 2 ［応答問題の解き方］

平叙文に答える問題

　設問が疑問文の形をしていない「平叙文」は、「疑問文」に対する「応答」のパターンではありませんので、あらゆる状況を考え、2人の関係性を想像します。なによりもまず、「会話の流れ」をとらえることが一番大切です。

🔊 68

3. Mark your answer on your answer sheet. 　Ⓐ Ⓑ Ⓒ

4. Mark your answer on your answer sheet. 　Ⓐ Ⓑ Ⓒ

5. Mark your answer on your answer sheet. 　Ⓐ Ⓑ Ⓒ

6. Mark your answer on your answer sheet. 　Ⓐ Ⓑ Ⓒ

Strategy for Part 3 ［会話問題の解き方］

図表を含む問題 ④

　図表を含む問題の図表には、一般的なメニュー、時刻表、表、グラフ以外にも、ホテルや企業の広告、社内の回覧など、独自のものが含まれています。図表の形などに惑わされずに、冷静に文字を見て、何について図表なのか、落ち着いて読み取りましょう。

Questions 7-9　　　　　　　　　　　　　　　　　　　🔊 69

Hiring Process

STEP 1 Create role openings and share the information	**STEP 2** Enter applicant data
STEP 3 Screen applicants for interviews and assessment	**STEP 4** Make offers to successful applicants
STEP 5 Request necessary documents and prepare the training schedule	

7. In which department does the man most likely belong to?
   (A) Human Resources
   (B) Marketing
   (C) Sales
   (D) Manufacturing

8. According to the woman, what type of employees does her department especially need?
   (A) Fresh graduates
   (B) Computer-savvy hires
   (C) Experienced in sales
   (D) Program managers

9. Look at the graphic. What will be the next step for the man to accomplish?
   (A) Step 2
   (B) Step 3
   (C) Step 4
   (D) Step 5

Part 4 Talks

Strategy for Part 4 ［説明文問題の解き方］

企業アナウンス ②

　アナウンスが流れたら、話し手と聞き手の関係をすぐに把握しましょう。日時や詳細内容には数字が含まれることが多いので、あらかじめ、設問と選択肢に目を通し、音声に出てくる数字の予測を立てておきましょう。

Questions 10-12　　　　　　　　　　　　　　　　　　🔊 70

10. How will the interview be conducted?

   (A) In one group

   (B) In two groups

   (C) In three groups

   (D) In four groups

11. According to the speaker, what will the staff member do?

   (A) Give the applicants a thumbs-up signal

   (B) Call the applicants' numbers

   (C) Get the applicant's card numbers

   (D) Monitor the applicants

12. According to the speaker, what must the applicants do after the interview?

   (A) Return to their seats

   (B) Thank the receptionist

   (C) Wait at the lobby

   (D) Give back the cards

Part 5 Incomplete Sentences

Strategy for Part 5 ［短文穴埋め問題の解き方］

【文法問題 ⑦　不定詞・動名詞】

　「不定詞・動名詞」の問題では、選択肢に to V と V-ing の両方が含まれている場合が多いため、常に**不定詞・動名詞のどちらを選択するか、正確に使い分ける必要**があります。ここで基本的な文法を学びましょう。

「不定詞の主な用法：to ＋動詞の原型」

　不定詞は、主語の人称や単数・複数に限定されず、動詞を主に以下の３つとして活用できる準動詞です。

① 名詞的用法「〜すること（は・を）」名詞と同じように、文中で主語・目的語・補語となる。

　例文 To be punctual is always important.「時間厳守であることは、常に重要である。」

② 形容詞的用法「〜するための・〜すべき○○」名詞を後ろから形容詞的に修飾する。

　例文 It is good to have friends to support you.「支えてくれる友を持つことは良いことです。」

③ 副詞的用法「〜するために・〜して…」副詞と同様に動詞・形容詞・副詞を修飾する。

　例文 The man gave up his career to be a writer.「その男性は作家になるために仕事をやめた。」

「不定詞」のみを目的語にとる動詞

　「未来的」という特徴を持ち、未達成の事柄が達成に向かうような未来達成的な性質を持ちます。
decide（決める）/ decline（断る）/ demand（要求する）/ desire（望む）/ determine（決心する）/ expect（予期する）/ hope（望む）/ manage（何とかやる）/ offer（申し出る）/ pretend（ふりする）/ promise（約束する）/ refuse（拒否する）/ resolve（決心する）/ wish（〜したいと思う）

「動名詞の主な用法：動詞の原型＋ ing」

動名詞は、動詞を ing 形に変換することで、名詞のように使うことができます。文中では、**主語・目的語（前置詞の目的語）・補語位置**に生起し、「〜すること」と訳します。

「動名詞」のみを目的語にとる動詞

　「実行済み・継続思考」という特徴を持ち、その動作や状態、行為に対して、どう思うのか、どういう行為を起こすのか、また、その動作の開始・終了・継続などについて表すことができます。
admit（認める）/ avoid（避ける）/ consider（熟考する）/ deny（否定する）/ enjoy（楽しむ）/ escape（免れる）/ finish（終える）/ imagine（想像する）/ mind（気にする）/ miss（しそこなう）/ practice（練習する）/ quit（やめる）/ suggest（提案する）/ recommend（薦める）

「不定詞と動名詞で意味が異なる動詞」

　中には、目的語位置に不定詞と動名詞のどちらを選ぶかによって文章全体の意味が変わってしまう動詞があります。次はその代表的な例です。**不定詞は『これからすること』、動名詞は『すでにしたこと』**と覚えておきましょう。

1. remember + to V 「（これから～することを）覚えている＝忘れずに～する」
   remember + V-ing 「（すでに～したことを）覚えている」
2. forget + to V 「（これから～することを）忘れる＝～し忘れる」
   forget + V-ing 「（すでに～したことを）忘れている」
3. stop + to V 「（これから～するために）立ち止まる」
   stop + V-ing 「（これまで～してきたことを）やめる」
4. regret + to V 「（これから～することを）残念に思う＝残念ながら～する」
   regret + V-ing 「（すでに～したことを）残念に思う＝～したのを後悔している」
5. try + to V 「（これから）～やろうとしてみる」
   try + V-ing 「（もうすでに・試しに）やった」

例題 A lot of corporations have succeeded at saving money by ------- travel costs.
   (A) reduces　　　　(B) reduce　　　　(C) reducing　　　　(D) reduction

解説 前置詞 by があり、動詞はそのままでは置けないので、前置詞の目的語になる動名詞にする必要があります。したがって、三単現の -s がついている (A) reduces と原形の (B) reduce は不正解。そして、空所の後ろには名詞句 travel costs とあるので、名詞 (D) reduction を置くことはできません。よって、(C) reducing が正解。動名詞を入れることで、名詞句 travel costs が動名詞の目的語となります。

参考訳 多くの企業が、旅費を抑えることで節約に成功してきた。

13. If there is any budget remaining in this month, we recommend ------- office supplies.
    (A) purchasing　　(B) purchase　　(C) purchased　　(D) to purchase

14. The final day for employees ------- their families for the annual Christmas party is today.
    (A) registering　　(B) resister　　(C) to register　　(D) registration

15. The company is set ------- a new hotel and condominium complex in Beijing.
    (A) developer　　(B) developing　　(C) developed　　(D) to develop

16. Act Global is a nationwide program that aims at ------- suitable internships for students.
    (A) to arrange　　(B) arranging　　(C) arrangements　　(D) arranges

17. Mr. Simons requested that one of his workers call the office supplier ------- about the availability and price ranges of its products.
    (A) inquiry　　(B) inquired　　(C) inquiring　　(D) to inquire

18. A trial medication used ------- common viral infections has proved to be effective.

(A) treated   (B) treatment   (C) treat   (D) to treat

19. Mr. Felix plays the piano and enjoys ------- his own tunes as a hobby on weekends.

(A) composes   (B) composing   (C) composer   (D) composed

20. In addition to ------- documents twice faster than the old model, this new copy machine is able to bind up books.

(A) copying   (B) copy   (C) copies   (D) copied

21. The furniture company has decided to expand its advertising budget ------- consumer awareness of its products by advertising them on TV commercials.

(A) raise   (B) raised   (C) to raise   (D) raising

Part 6   Text Completion

Strategy for Part 6 [長文穴埋め問題の解き方]

　Part 6 の「文脈に沿って解く設問」の中で、選択肢がすべて 1 つの文になっている「文選択問題」は、その問題だけを考えていると、時間がかかってしまいます。ほかの問題を解きながら、その「文選択問題」に向けて全体の方向性を考えておき、最後に全外の流れを抑えてから「文選択問題」を解答することをお勧めします。

Question 22-25 refer to the following e-mail.

Date: April 1
To: All New Employees
From: Sara Brockman <s.brockman.it@wilcom.com>

Dear everyone,

Welcome to Wilcom Industries!

I would like to ------- each one of you for passing your interviews, and we all look
22.
forward to working with you from this day forward.

With regards to your training schedule, please be reminded that your first day ------ 23. on April 3rd. We will be orienting you on the organization structure and give you a tour around the various departments to ------ you. Kindly see the attached file for 24. the schedule and information for this week. ------. 25.

I will be personally handling your orientation on the first day, and I look forward to seeing you.

Best Regards,

Sara Brockman
HR Manager, Wilcom Industries

22. (A) commend   (B) comment   (C) congratulate   (D) comfort

23. (A) was scheduled   (B) is scheduled   (C) schedules   (D) had scheduled

24. (A) introduce   (B) imitate   (C) improve   (D) intend

25. (A) If you have any questions before the training, you may forward them to me.
    (B) Please don't arrive too early at the training room.
    (C) Make sure to remember the faces of all the persons in each department.
    (D) Remember to bring water and lunch for the training session.

| **Strategy for Part 7** ［読解問題の解き方］ |

　Reading Section の解答時間は 75 分と限られているので、トリプル・パッセージの 15 問すべてを解くとなると時間が足りないと思う受験者も多いでしょう。しかしトリプル・パッセージの設問は難問ばかりではありません。それぞれのパッセージのつながりを意識して、3 つの文書から全体の流れを読み取りましょう。

Questions 26 to 30 refer to the following two e-mails.

Date: March 25
To: Masayoshi Takeda <m.takeda@lylestudios.com>
From: Hannah Cavill <h.cavill@lylestudios.com>
Subject: Marketing Plan Checklist for April

Dear Mr. Takeda,

I have prepared the Marketing Plan Checklist for the next three months. I apologize for making you wait as it was already due last Friday on the 22nd, and I appreciate you extending the deadline to today. I used a similar format to the one that we used last January, so as to keep the uniformity of our documents.

If you have any concerns about the checklist, I would be happy to answer your query and do any revision needed as soon as possible.

Kind regards,

Hannah Cavill
Staff, Lyle Studios

Date: March 25
To: Hannah Cavill <h.cavill@lylestudios.com>
From: Masayoshi Takeda <m.takeda@lylestudios.com>
Subject: Re: Marketing Plan Checklist for April

Dear Ms. Cavill,

Thank you for sending the file. I understand that you are currently handling three other projects at the same time, and I hope you can submit your deliverables much more on schedule in the future. I have gone over the checklist and everything seems okay, except that you have included a billboard rental for the first month. I believe that we have discussed this matter in the last meeting, and that this might not be a plausible idea early on since we are working on a limited budget. I have edited the file and placed this item to two months from now, so you can now send this to the team for their compliance.

26. When was the original deadline for Ms. Cavill?
(A) Last Thursday
(B) Last Friday
(C) Last Saturday
(D) Last Sunday

27. In paragraph 2, line 2 of the Ms. Cavill's email, the word "query" has the closest meaning to
(A) comment
(B) problem
(C) question
(D) concern

28. What does Mr. Takeda hope Ms. Cavill will do in the future?
(A) Improve her proposals
(B) Fix the schedules
(C) Submit documents on time
(D) Allocate a bigger budget

29. What might not be a feasible idea?
(A) Leasing an advertising board on the first month
(B) Organizing a magazine photoshoot on the third month
(C) Scouting for new models
(D) Portfolio Management

30. To which month was the proposal moved to?
(A) February
(B) April
(C) May
(D) July

Mini Test

🎧 Listening Section

Part 1 Photographs

1.

🔊 71

Ⓐ Ⓑ Ⓒ Ⓓ

2.

Ⓐ Ⓑ Ⓒ Ⓓ

3.

Ⓐ Ⓑ Ⓒ Ⓓ

4.

Ⓐ Ⓑ Ⓒ Ⓓ

Part 2 Question-Response

5. Mark your answer on your answer sheet.　　Ⓐ Ⓑ Ⓒ　　🔊 72

6. Mark your answer on your answer sheet.　　Ⓐ Ⓑ Ⓒ

7. Mark your answer on your answer sheet.　　Ⓐ Ⓑ Ⓒ

8. Mark your answer on your answer sheet.　　Ⓐ Ⓑ Ⓒ　　🔊 73

9. Mark your answer on your answer sheet.　　Ⓐ Ⓑ Ⓒ

10. Mark your answer on your answer sheet.　　Ⓐ Ⓑ Ⓒ

11. What do the men say they are already accustomed to?
    (A) Checking wirings
    (B) Commuting in fast-paced environments
    (C) Traveling in various weather conditions
    (D) Catching mice

12. Why are the men visiting the office?
    (A) To install pipes
    (B) To fix computers
    (C) To inspect faulty wires
    (D) To renovate the conference room

13. What does the woman say the men may find?
    (A) Hidden passages
    (B) Employees working from home
    (C) Other things that need repair
    (D) Cracked ceilings

Part 4 **Talks**

Questions 14-16   🔊 75

BOOK CONVENTION

DAY 1

8:00 am – Opening Ceremony

9:00 am – Fiction Author Panel

11:00 am – E-books Seminar

1:00 pm – Patenting and Book Publicity Forum

K & A Publishing House

14. Where is the talk most likely taking place?
- (A) At a library
- (B) At a publishing company
- (C) At a bookstore
- (D) At a newspaper company

15. Look at the graphic. Which session are the listeners required to attend?
- (A) Opening Ceremony
- (B) Fiction Author Panel
- (C) E-books Seminar
- (D) Patenting and Book Publicity Forum

16. What still needs to be confirmed?
- (A) The event location
- (B) The catering arrangements
- (C) The start time
- (D) The program

Part 5 **Incomplete Sentences**

Strategy for Part 5 ［短文穴埋め問題の解き方］

【実践演習】
　これまで学んできたことを活かして実践問題を 10 問解いてみましょう。間違えた問題や解くのに時間がかかってしまった問題は、それぞれの UNIT でもう一度確認しましょう。

17. The travel agency is expecting a severe decline in tourism this year ------- plans to hold an international event, which will attract thousands.

(A) otherwise　　(B) despite　　(C) according　　(D) whenever

18. The position of sales manager is open only to ------- who have worked for the company for five or more years.

(A) employing　　(B) employment　　(C) employed　　(D) employees

19. The letter of praise ------- Mr. Waltz, a store director, received from a customer has been forwarded to the head quarter.

(A) that　　(B) what　　(C) in which　　(D) of which

20. After several minor changes were made to the proposal, Mr. Kazi scheduled a meeting with ------- staff.

(A) him　　(B) he　　(C) himself　　(D) his

21. One of our restaurant attendants ------- glad to assist the company's CEO with his seat.

(A) were being　　(B) would be　　(C) is being　　(D) have been

22. Inquiries ------- to medical insurance should be directed to the Human Resources Department.

(A) pertains　　(B) pertaining　　(C) pertain　　(D) pertained

23. ------- its 10th anniversary, the company is planning to hold a special event for all of its employees, including full- and part-time employees.

(A) Celebrates　　(B) In celebration　　(C) Celebration　　(D) To celebrate

24. One of the famous destinations is Ashikaga Flower Park, ------- visitors can enjoy the most beautiful wisteria and ice creams with the flavor of the flower in April and May.

(A) which   (B) where   (C) that   (D) when

25. When buying a new smartphone, customers are definitely encouraged to compare products and prices before making ------- final decision.

(A) them   (B) theirs   (C) their   (D) themselves

26. Due to the pavement construction, detour signs will be ------- placed along the main route to the national art museum.

(A) prominently   (B) markedly   (C) importantly   (D) observantly

Questions 27-30 refer to the following e-mail.

To: All employees
From: Emmanuel Garezza
Date: 16 September
Subject: New Employee Guide Training

R&K Industries has recently updated its employee guide. -------. Although the **27.** information concerning benefits and employment terms have been retained, some other important revisions have been made. This version of the guide includes new policies related to e-mail privacy, internet use, and use of company phones. Our travel guidelines have also been -------. The reimbursement process after a trip has **28.** been made much more efficient using an online system which our IT Department completed last month.

All employees must attend an informational session about the policies. One-hour sessions will be held at 9:00 A.M. on September 20 and September 30. -------, **29.** employees will be requested to sign a form to acknowledge that they have received, read, and understood the information contained in our handbook, and that the terms have been accepted. Please arrange with your manager ------- one of these **30.** sessions.

Emmanuel Garezza

27. (A) Thank you for complying with the policies.
    (B) A new logo is displayed on the front page of the book.
    (C) This is the first change in ten years.
    (D) Corporate lawyers have been consulted to revise it.

28. (A) revised
    (B) removed
    (C) disclosed
    (D) notified

29. (A) All in all
    (B) On the other hand
    (C) Contrary
    (D) Right afterwards

30. (A) to attend
    (B) who attended
    (C) while attending
    (D) in attendance

Questions 31-35 refer to the following e-mail.

To: k.westbay@stanion.com
From: n.kim@kroppel.com
Subject: Follow up

Dear Kara,

I hope you were able to find time to review the budget I sent last Wednesday. As you can see from the document, we are looking to spend Stanion's production money as sparingly as possible. —[1]—. We also hope you found the repayment terms within reason. —[2]—. After the $1.5 million debt is settled, the 60-40 split (60 percent for Kroppel Productions and 40 percent for Stanion) we are proposing should be profitable for both companies.

To update you on pre-production, our location scout has found several ideal spots in Russia. —[3]—. Our third main lead will be portrayed by Sergey Fedorov, a prominent indie actor, and a close friend of the director.

Speaking of the director, Andrey has asked that the number of products being featured in the film be kept low. —[4]—. He doesn't want to give the audience the impression that the movie was created to be a means to advertise explicitly.

Let me know your thoughts, and let's talk soon.

Nathalie Kim
Development Head
Kroppel Productions

31. Who most likely is Kara Westbay?
    (A) A scriptwriter
    (B) An upcoming actress
    (C) An executive producer
    (D) A film director

32. What can be inferred about the film?
    (A) The film is aimed at German audiences.
    (B) Sergey Fedorov will not be paid by the director.
    (C) Kroppel Productions is Russian company.
    (D) It targets audience of the indie industry.

33. What does Nathalie say would give the impression that the movie means to advertise explicitly?
    (A) Having excessive product placement
    (B) Getting sponsorships from companies
    (C) Selling merchandise related to the movie
    (D) Focusing less on the chosen actors

34. In paragraph 1, line 3, the word "sparingly" has the closest meaning to
    (A) carefully
    (B) excessively
    (C) lavishly
    (D) confidently

35. In which of the positions marked [1], [2], [3], and [4] does the following sentence best belong?

    "We've cast two Russian unknowns in the lead roles who show potential."

    (A) [1]
    (B) [2]
    (C) [3]
    (D) [4]

Illustrations & Photos

著　者
松本恵美子（まつもと えみこ）　順天堂大学講師
井上健人（いのうえ けんと）　神田外語大学語学専任講師
Graciella Bautista（グラシエラ・バウティスタ）

800点を目指す TOEIC® L&R TEST 演習

2023 年 2 月 20 日　　第 1 版発行
2024 年 3 月 20 日　　第 4 版発行

著　者　　松本恵美子・井上健人・Graciella Bautista
発行者　　前田俊秀
発行所　　株式会社　三修社
　　　　　〒 150-0001 東京都渋谷区神宮前 2-2-22
　　　　　TEL 03-3405-4511　　FAX 03-3405-4522
　　　　　振替 00190-9-72758
　　　　　https://www.sanshusha.co.jp
　　　　　編集担当 三井るり子・伊藤宏実
印刷・製本　日経印刷株式会社

©2023 Printed in Japan ISBN978-4-384-33521-7 C1082
表紙デザイン―峯岸孝之
本文デザイン & DTP―Shibasaki Rie
準拠音声録音―ELEC
準拠音声製作―高速録音株式会社

教科書準拠 CD 発売
本書の準拠 CD をご希望の方は弊社までお問い合わせください。